BILLIE AND THE BOYS

By

Hal Shearon McBride, Jr.

Billie
And The Boys

Hal Shearon McBride, Jr.

A Memoir

Other Books by the Author

To Bear Witness: A Memoir (2009)

Who Be Dragons: A Historical Novel (2010)

McBride, Hal (1937-)

Billie and the Boys/ Hal McBride

1.Flagstaff, Arizona 2. Arizona State College now Northern Arizona University 3. Stigler, Oklahoma 4.Tulsa, Oklahoma 5. Family stories 6. Christmas stories 7. 1960s 8. Oak Creek Canyon 9. Navajo Reservation 10. Glen Canyon Dam 12. Northern Arizona 13. Eastern Oklahoma 14. 1950s 15. Baseball

"Billie and the Boys," by Hal Shearon McBride Jr.. ISBN 978-1-60264-746-6.

Published 2011 by Virtualbookworm.com Publishing Inc., P.O. Box 9949, College Station, TX 77842, US. ©2011, Hal Shearon McBride Jr. All rights reserved. No part of this publication may be reproduced, stored in a retrieval system, or transmitted in any form or by any means, electronic, mechanical, recording or otherwise, without the prior written permission of Hal Shearon McBride Jr.

Manufactured in the United States of America.

Dedications

For our family:

David Grant
James Michael
Cheryl Ann
Emily Ann
Amanda Jean
William Michael
And
Buddy
(Dason Alderidge)

TABLE OF CONTENTS

Principal Characters	1
AUTHOR'S NOTE	10
Necessary Knowledge	12
A Different Kind of Dirt	15
Student Athletes	25
Cottage City 1958	29
The Weatherford Hotel	33
Summer Guests	43
Road Trips	47
Oak Creek in August	52
Meanwhile, Back in Stigler	55
The Deep Woods	57
Christmas 1958	60
The Stormy Road Home	75
Home Again	79
April 1959	84
Cottonseed Hulls	90
Summer Visitors	95
Northeraire	97
H & H Wholesale	102
The Reservation	105
Gone to Town	113
Jimmy the Greek	117
Alums	121
Time to Go	126
Took Us Back to Tulsa	130
Jay Boy	135
Oiler Baseball	141
A Home of Our Own	143
November 22, 1963	147
Silver Bells	150
The Boys and Baseball	154
Cascia Hall	161

Vivian and Hubert Claunts – 1950

PRINCIPAL CHARACTERS

OKLAHOMA

Claunts, Hubert (1894 to 1990) – Husband to Vivian Pearl Lane Claunts, Father to H. B. "Boots" Claunts and Rupert (John) "Tag" Claunts, Uncle to the author and co-owner of the Stigler 5 & Up.

Claunts, H. B. "Boots" (1919-) – Eldest son of Hubert and Vivian Lane Claunts, married Jackie Riley Claunts in February of 1942, World War II veteran.

Claunts, Jackie Riley – daughter of depression era Stigler merchants, buyer for Goldwater's in the Arizona Biltmore, and wife of Boots Claunts.

Claunts, (Rupert) John Wesley "Tag" (1920-1992) – youngest son of Hubert and Vivian Lane Claunts.

Claunts, Vivian Pearl (Lane) (1902 to 1966) – Wife to Hubert Claunts, Mother to H. B. "Boots" Claunts and Rupert (John) "Tag" Claunts, Eldest sister to Follie Belle (Lane) McBride, Aunt to the author and co-owner of the Stigler 5 & Up.

Cundiff, Anna Lee (McBride) (1920 – 2008) – Wife to Ellsworth Cundiff, youngest child of J. H. and Annie McBride, mother to Ellsworth Cundiff, Jr. and Billie Ann (Cundiff) Bellner and Aunt to the author.
Davidson, L. J. – Retired Dentist in Memphis, Tennessee, classmate and friend of the author's parents, Army Air Corps pilot during World War II and following the publication of To Bear Witness a friend to the author.
Farmer, Lela Jean (Reynolds) – Sister to Jay Reynolds, Wife to Ray Farmer, Southwestern Bell operator and Executive Secretary at Oklahoma Nursing Home Supply.
Farmer, Ray – Sallisaw merchant (Western Auto), Husband to Lela Jean (Reynolds) Farmer, Army Air Force Veteran of World War II, brother-in-law to Jay Reynolds.
Hamill, William A. (Bill) (1937-) – Cascia Hall, Football coach in 1964, Director of Studies 1972-1997, Augustinian Priest and Ph.D., present member of the faculty at The University of Tulsa and a close friend to the author.
Harris, Elgin – Baseball Coach and mentor to David and Michael McBride.
LaFave, Eulis – Manager of Hays and Buchanan, Stigler, Oklahoma. An honorable man, a friend to the author and to his Grandfather.
Lane, Marvella Hammock (Mema Lane) (1882 to 1978) – Wife of Oscar Breckinridge Lane, Mother to Vivian Pearl Lane Claunts, Lacy Leo Lane, Ruth Lane Lightfoot, Archie Jimmy Lane and Follie Belle Lane McBride and maternal Grandmother to the author.
Lane, Oscar Breckinridge (1882 to 1938) – Husband to Marvella Hammock Lane, Father to Vivian Pearl Lane Claunts, Lacy Leo Lane, Ruth Lane Lightfoot, Archie Jimmy Lane, Follie Belle Lane McBride and maternal Grandfather to the author.
Martin, Billie Jean – See Billie Jean McBride.
Martin, Ezra Thomas (1902-1952) – Father to Billie Jean (Martin) McBride, Lou Martin Mattox, Annice Martin Reynolds and Pauline Martin Ross, auto mechanic in Vian, Oklahoma.
Martin, Lou Elba – See Lou Elba Mattox.

Martin (later Merriott, later Hunt), Mary Dale Sells (1911-2004) – Mother to Billie Jean Martin McBride, Lou Martin Mattox, Annice Martin Reynolds, Pauline Martin Ross, Michael Merriott and Warner Merriott.

Martin, Pauline – See Pauline Ross.

Martin, Sarah Annice – See Sarah Annice Reynolds.

Mattox, Charles – Sallisaw, Oklahoma entrepreneur, Husband to Lou Elba (Martin) Mattox, Brother-in-Law to Billie Jean (Martin) McBride and to the author, Billie Jean Martin McBride resided in the Mattox home from 5th grade until our marriage in their home, Father to Paul David Mattox and Brent Alan Mattox, Navy veteran of World War II, Brother-in-Law to Billie and Hal McBride.

Mattox (Martin), Lou Elba (1930-) – Eldest sister of Billie Martin McBride, Wife to Charles Mattox, Billie Jean Martin McBride resided in the Mattox home from 5th grade until our marriage in their home, Mother to Paul David Mattox and Brent Alan Mattox, Sister-in-Law to the author.

McBride, Anna Lee – See Anna Lee Cundiff.

McBride, Annie Gorman (Wood) (Mema Mac) (1890-1962) – Wife of James Howett McBride, Mother of James Howett McBride (Jr.), Sherwell McBride Timmons, Hal Shearon McBride, Sr. and Anna Lee McBride Cundiff and Paternal Grandmother to the author.

McBride, Billie Jean (Martin) (1938-) – Wife to Hal Shearon McBride, Jr., Mother to David Grant McBride and James Michael McBride and "One of those pretty little Martin girls" (Lou, Annice, Pauline and Billie)

McBride, Cheryl Ann (Barnett) (1961-) – Wife to James Michael McBride.

McBride, David Grant (1957-) – Eldest son of Billie Jean McBride and Hal S. McBride, Jr.

McBride, Follie Belle (Lane) (1918-2003) – Wife of H. Shearon McBride, Sr., Mother to Hal S. McBride, Jr. and James Lane McBride, Youngest daughter of O.B. and Marvella Lane, and served as Haskell County Tag Agent and Secretary of the Haskell County Election Board. (Mother)

McBride, Hal Shearon Sr. (1916-1993) – Husband to Follie Belle Lane McBride, Father to Hal S. McBride, Jr. and James Lane McBride, Youngest son of J. H. and Annie McBride and owner of McBride Radio and Television, Stigler, Oklahoma. (Dad)

McBride, Hal Shearon Jr. (1937-) – Husband to Billie Jean Martin McBride, Father to David Grant McBride and James Michael McBride, Eldest son of Follie Belle and H. Shearon McBride, Sr. and author of this memoir.

McBride, James Howett (Sr.) (1888-1957) – Husband to Annie Gorman McBride, Father to J. Howett McBride, Sherwell McBride Timmons, Hal Shearon McBride, Sr. and Anna Lee McBride Cundiff, Operator of Hays and Buchanan Dry Goods and Paternal Grandfather to the author. (Bepa Mac, Mr. Mac)

McBride, James Lane (1940-1987) – Husband to Wilma Lee Sunday McBride, Father to Shari Lynn McBride Malthaner and Sandy Lee McBride Brewer, Youngest son of H. Shearon McBride and Follie Belle McBride and brother to the author.

McBride, James Michael (1959-) – Youngest son of Billie Jean McBride and Hal S. McBride, Jr.

McBride, Wilma Lee (Sunday) – Widow of James Lane McBride and Sister-in-Law to the author.

Reynolds, Sarah Annice (Martin) (1931-2010) – Sister to Billie Jean (Martin) McBride, Wife to Jay Reynolds, Mother to Freddie Reynolds (deceased), Karen Sue (Reynolds) Wampler and Barbara Ann Reynolds (deceased), Sister-in-Law to the author.

Reynolds, Frederick Jay (1924-1995) – Husband to Sarah Annice (Martin) Reynolds, Father to Freddie Reynolds (deceased), Karen Sue (Reynolds) Wampler and Barbara Ann Reynolds (deceased), a career Southwestern Bell employee, Sallisaw City Commissioner, Navy veteran of World War II. Brother-in-Law to Billie and Hal McBride.

Reynolds (Martin, Hickman), Barbara Ann – Youngest child of Frederick Jay and Annice Martin Reynolds.

Reynolds, Freddie (1949-2009) – Eldest child of Frederick Jay and Annice Martin Reynolds.

Reynolds (Wampler), Karen Sue – Eldest daughter of Frederick Jay and Annice Martin Reynolds.

Ross, James Bernard (1932-2005) – Husband to Pauline Martin Ross, Vian, Co-owner Ross Brothers Store, Vian, Oklahoma.

Ross, Pauline (Martin) (1933-2003) – Sister to Billie Jean (Martin) McBride, Wife to Bernard Ross, Mother to Debra Ross Anderson, Jimmie Lou Ross Eubanks and James Martin Ross, Registered Nurse and graduate of the St. Edwards School of Nursing, Fort Smith, Arkansas, School Nurse Vian, Oklahoma Public Schools, Sister-in-Law to the author.

Thomas, James William "Jimmy" (1937-2010) – Childhood neighbor and lifelong friend to the author.

ARIZONA

Andrews, Ira – 1958 teammate at Arizona State College and friend to the author.

Donnelley, Thorne – Retired resident of Northernaire, Munds Park, Arizona during the summer of 1959.

Goldwater, Barry (1909-1989) – United States Senator representing the State of Arizona and a frequent guest at Northernaire, Munds Park, Arizona during the summer of 1959.

Gregg, Herbert – Head Basketball Coach at Arizona State College from 1950 to 1974 amassing 290 victories.

Grey, Richard -- Manager of Northernaire Country Club (now Pinewood Country Club), Munds Park, Arizona in 1959.

Haines, Connie – Wife of Lamar Haines, Cottage City neighbor, teacher in Flagstaff Public Schools and friend.

Haines, Lamar (1927-1986) – Husband of Connie Haines, Cottage City neighbor, Wilson Sporting Goods Representative, teacher, coach and athletic director in the Flagstaff Public Schools, guide, hunter, outdoor chef/camp cook and friend to the author.

Hall, Ann – Owner of the Weatherford Hotel during the 1950's and 1960's.

Herbert, Ralph – Partner in H&H Wholesale Grocery, Flagstaff

Herrera, Arnold – Partner in H&H Wholesale Grocery, Flagstaff

Hicks, Alfred – Cottage City neighbor, Arizona Educator and Navajo artist.

Hicks, Sally – Cottage City neighbor, wife to Alfred Hicks.

Jimmy the Greek – Owner of a small café in Winslow, Arizona.

Lansing, Brownie – Cottage City neighbor, Arizona educator with earned doctorate from Northern Arizona University, close friend to the author.

Lansing, Paul – Cottage City neighbor, Faculty of Northern Arizona University with earned doctorate from The University of Wisconsin, close friend to the author.

Maddox, Hosie (1938 - 1992) – Student athlete at Arizona State College, Member of the University Athletic Hall of Fame and friend to the author.

McCormick, Bill – Student athlete at Arizona State College, husband to Nancy McCormick, Salesman for Friends Office Supply in Flagstaff and friend to the author.

Randolph, Earl "Randy" – Student athlete at Arizona State College and friend to the author.

Spilsbury, Max – Head Football coach at Arizona State College compiling a record of 58-25-5.

1966 REED FOOTBALL STEELERS

Standing from the left: Richie Atterberry, Vic Harris, Hal McBride, David McBride, Mark Dees, Jack Ellison, Joe Banasky
Kneeling from the left: Greg Morris, Doug Swyden, Kevin Eidson, Timmy McWilliams, Steve Breshears, Bill Vining
Not Pictured: Jay Pancoast, Mark Shelton

1963 EAST CENTRAL STEELERS BASEBALL

1969 SALLISAW (FARMER-O'NEAL FORD) BASEBALL ROSTER

Corley, Cary
Davis, Joe David
Flute, George
Fogg, Ricky Joe
Hight, Mike
Lancaster, Larry
Marvin, Wayne
McBride, David

McBride, Mike
McCormick, Keith
Nowlin, Bill
Parsons, Steve (Super Chicken)
Rhodes, Phillip
Sossamon, Steve
Vann, Ferris

SALLISAW GRADE SCHOOL BASKETBALL 1967-69

Kneeling from the left: Mike McBride, Phillip Rhodes, Mike Ellis, David McBride, Bill Nowlin, Burn Collins, Kevin Bateman, Joe David Davis, William White.

Standing for the left: Patrick Pointer, Larry Lancaster, Steve Sossaman, Wayne Marvin, Carey Corley, Gary Boyd, Mike Hight.

Standing Behind: Hal McBride

FAMILY OF J.H. AND ANNIE McBRIDE – 1949

From the left: Shearon, Sherwell, J.H, Annie, Howett and Anna Lee

AUTHOR'S NOTE

This memoir is a collection of family stories set in eastern Oklahoma and northern Arizona. It is not a time frame chronology of events.

The Stigler, Sallisaw, and Vian of our formative years gave Billie and me a sense of rootedness and an ethical foundation. Flagstaff is a physical location and a pleasant ideation of our independent beginnings together. Tulsa is our home.

I remember being young. It was a time when my full orientation was directed toward family and future; the world seemed filled with endless possibilities. In part I write collections of stories such as these because I am reluctant to release those beliefs. I need to judge my world and my life as a continual stream of opportunities if I but have the astuteness to recognize them.

While in candor, I must acknowledge diminished physical agility and arthritis are clear and present reminders that aging is a physical experience as well as a state of mind. However, it is the capacity to appreciate most of life's vibrations that carries the reminders of the unbridled optimism of my youth. The evolution of an idea or cognitive concept still invigorates me and provides the resolve to convert the ideations into actions.

Such ideations should not be allowed to remain passive flights of the imagination, but rather should be compelled to leave that inert state and be driven into activity. Then, a tangible outcome can be derived and we can retain a reasonable command of our lives.

In this case, a collection of words is organized in such a fashion that it comes to comprise a collection of stories. These stories become a book. Ultimately, the paper upon which the stories are written will yellow and its fibers will unravel, but the words will remain as fresh as the day they escaped the writer's mind.

There is a philosophy of competition that espouses that the participant must possess the will to push through fatigue and discomfort, allowing the final measures of ability and stamina to be consumed by the endeavor. Should the capacity of the contestant to complete the competition be found lacking, the final outcome will be unsatisfactory and will expose an unappealing frailty. It is these experiences, in competition and in life, that teach us and toughen us.

There is little worse than to have never competed, to have never risked failure in the pursuit of a prized dream.

So, I will organize my words, fashion my stories, and be amazed when a book emerges. When this collection is done, I shall begin another.

In this writing, it perplexed me that I can remember certain events with great clarity while other occurrences that I believe I should recall completely elude me.

These stories are true to my very best recollections and any errors in the manuscript are solely mine.

NECESSARY KNOWLEDGE

In almost every way, this writing must be considered as an extension of To Bear Witness, so its genesis must also be considered as rooted in the curiosity of my eldest granddaughter, Emily Ann McBride Tichenor.

I know now that the reasons I chose to write To Bear Witness and now Billie and the Boys are clearly the thoughts I recorded in the Prologue of that first work. I feel that somewhere in this paragraph my motives are captured.

Perhaps, as some veteran is said to have observed, "They are only lost when no one remembers them." I feel the need to make an effort to see that at least the essence of those to whom I am so indebted is sustained in the cognitive network of our evolving family; preventing them from completely vanishing into the abyss of obscurity to which we are prone to allow those who comprise our family histories to become assigned.

Since I am not so foolhardy as to believe that everyone who might read this accounting will also have read the first memoir, I will provide the outline of necessary knowledge from the first work.

I was born Hal Shearon McBride, Jr. in February of 1937 to Hal Shearon McBride, Sr. and Follie Belle Lane McBride in the rural southern Oklahoma community of Stigler in an area commonly referred to as "Little Dixie." Oklahoma had not yet been a state for thirty years.

Mother's nickname was Jinkie. Daddy's nickname was Poo. I was Jinky Poo until I started school. It is reported that at that time my Mother insisted, by accounts very adamantly and relentlessly, that I be called Hal.

My paternal grandparents were James Howett McBride and Annie Woods McBride. Granddaddy McBride operated Hays and Buchanan, a local dry goods store. As with many of his generation, my father was absent from my life during the World War II years. Then, when I was twelve, my grandfather employed me in his store. He became a profound core influence in my life. I admired him greatly and loved him dearly.

My maternal grandparents were Oscar Breckinridge Lane and Marvella Hammock Lane. Granddaddy Lane was an Ozark Mountain farmer until his death shortly after my birth. As a result, my Grandmother Lane came to live in Stigler with her eldest daughter and her husband, Hubert and Vivian Lane Claunts. My Uncle Hubert and Aunt Vivian operated the Stigler 5 & Up.

There were four children in my Father's family. The eldest was James Howett, followed by Sherwell (Timmons), then my father and the baby, Anna Lee (Cundiff).

There were five children in my Mother's family. The eldest was Vivian, followed by Lacey, Ruth (Lightfoot), Archie, and my Mother was the baby.

I was born into the Great Depression, perhaps not at its peak, but it was far from waning. I was almost five years old when Pearl Harbor was bombed and my early school years were during World War II.

I grew up in the midst of people who had chosen to remain in rural Oklahoma during the Great Depression. They labored and sacrificed to hold on to their stores and to their land, to somehow simply survive – and survive they did.

They were a stubborn, proud, and pragmatic group who weathered the depression and the onslaughts of nature. I know that the character of this determined and optimistic merchant class that once dotted the rural southern plains profoundly influenced me.

The most significant single event in my life occurred on November 21, 1956 in Sallisaw, Oklahoma. Billie Jean Martin and I were married.

These memoirs reflect not only the experiences of my family, but each with their own personal variations, the stories of almost all of my classmates at Stigler High School in the 1950's.

The stories that have been so graciously shared since the publication of <u>To Bear Witness</u> served to further convince me that each of us have our stories to tell. The diverse manners in which these stories traveled to me further convinced me that we are not cognitively static. The stories interested me, the story tellers deeply influenced me.

We share the truly significant human and soulful essentials.

CHAPTER ONE

A Different Kind of Dirt.

"Just what kind of dirt is this?" Billie asked.

My wife stood in the doorway of our new home on the campus of Arizona State College in Flagstaff, pointing with the small potting shovel she held in her right hand into the small flower pot she carried.

She had gone outside the unit to collect a little dirt so she could plant a flower in the unit. She returned with a pot containing a substance quite foreign to us.

I looked at the pot filled with odd pox-marked grainy red pebbles and said, "I don't know."

It was our first night alone in Flagstaff, my parents having departed from southern Arizona and a visit with relatives, Boots and Jackie Claunts, before returning to Oklahoma. I was unwilling to commit as to the disappointing contents of the flower pot. I did know it wasn't soil from the Canadian River bottoms.

Upon closer examination, Billie and I agreed that any flowers with which we were familiar were unlikely to grow in that soil. Growing anything in Flagstaff would prove to be quite different from any cultivation to which we were accustomed.

Over the following months, we discovered northern Arizona possessed a number of fundamental ecological and environmental variances from our native eastern Oklahoma. Some were good, some were bad, but all were interesting.

Billie quickly resolved the flower pot dilemma with a bag of potting soil from the local five and dime. She had her flowers, but the very idea of buying dirt in a bag stuck in her craw for a bit.

We still laugh about gathering up the red volcanic cinders for planting flowers.

Billie and the Boys

The previous week I had buried my Grandmother McBride's kitchen scraps in her yard with a posthole digger. The memory gave me pause as I reflected on the disposal of garbage in such unresponsive soil. Then I realized even had the soil been more pliable, I had no posthole diggers.

I do on occasion still wonder if the coffee grounds my Grandmother collected for separate burial really did attract earthworms as my Grandfather asserted.

The landscape of northern Arizona was nothing like I had expected. Flagstaff was not a desert town, but rather a mountain community. The campus was dotted with large ponderosa pines, spruce, and aspens. With their grayish white bark, the aspens were unique. Their leaves gone for the winter, black abstract lines flowed across the bark as if drawn by pen and ink. The black lines suggested an organization, some grand plan, but no matter how closely you examined the geometric designs, no such repetitive configuration was discernable.

As you looked toward the mountains to the north, groves of aspens seemed to punctuate the mountain sides. The slopes were otherwise green until the snow capped San Francisco Peaks emerged from the tree line.

It was far removed from the sand and cactus that I had envisioned.

In December of 1957, Billie and I found few initial similarities between Flagstaff and Stigler. I don't believe we were making many overt comparisons. As the variations gradually revealed themselves, the differences turned out to be stimulating, enriching, and at times quite challenging. Life in Flagstaff was going to get our best efforts.

My parents, Shearon and Follie McBride, had helped us move a thousand miles west of our native eastern Oklahoma. All of our transportable goods were carried in a small hand-crafted trailer borrowed from a friend of my dad. The trailer was towed behind their black and white 1957 Plymouth station wagon.

Unit number 85 in Cottage City on the campus of Arizona State College was the primary staging area for our newest endeavor. Cottage City, the campus housing for married students, was originally constructed to provide temporary housing for officer training candidates during World War II. The units were retained to accommodate the flood of married World War II veterans who had chosen to take full advantage of their benefits under the GI Bill. They were followed by the veterans of the Korean War or conflict or police action or whatever politically correct term was being applied at the time. The GI Bill was seen by most of these veterans, all depression era children ushered into adulthood by conflict, as a path to a better life through education.

As the roads departed the main campus and entered Cottage City, the pavement ceased and the road became red volcanic cinder, the quality of which seemed to reinforce the temporary intention with which these structures were originally assembled.

By 1958, these one bedroom frame buildings had become home to yet another generation of married students. They were painted wooden structures whose interior walls were so thin that you did not have to guess what your neighbors were having for dinner. We would rapidly learn you could knock on the wall and conduct most necessary communication.

While the prevailing color of Cottage City was battleship gray, young couple after young couple painted the interior walls with more pleasing colors. To cover the cold wooden floors, they bought inexpensive 9x12 rugs with rubber backing from Sears and Roebuck or JC Penny stores in downtown Flagstaff. These inexpensive rugs covered the floor of the living room area so completely that the illusion of wall to wall carpeting was created. We bought such a rug.

There was a large vented gas space heater located between the living area and the kitchen. The units were adequately drafty to alleviate any concerns about air quality.

The bathroom was just off the kitchen. There was no door knob, but rather a rope had been run through the opening and knotted on both sides. While not esthetically pleasing, it was functional. There was only a shower, but the water pressure from the shower head was strong. Billie was satisfied or at least accepting.

Billie and the Boys

The unit came with a twin bed in the living room area, a chrome dinette with three or four chairs, a small gas cooking stove, and a double bed in the bedroom.

The rent was forty dollars a month with all utilities paid.

The door into the living room was the only entry. There was a small front porch with a clothes line strung from the exterior wall to a porch post. In a Flagstaff winter with a north facing unit, any clothing hung on the line promptly froze. We retrieved diapers that had frozen stiff until neighbors showed us about placing a wooden clothes rack on top of the heater.

As I now write this, it sounds like risky behavior. But we had been using a similar clothes rack over my parent's floor furnace before leaving Stigler. We placed a high priority on warm, clean, dry diapers.

Yes, the diapers were cloth – use, place in a plastic diaper pail with a bit of cleansing mixture, then wash, dry, fold, and reuse.

Formula was mixed, boiled, and poured into glass bottles that had been prepared in a bottle sterilizer on the stove top. The filled bottles were placed in the refrigerator to be stored until needed. Then a bottle would be re-heated in a sauce pan of water on the stove top and served when you could no longer feel the warmed liquid sprinkled on your wrist.

We had a high chair, a crib, a rocking chair, a stroller, and what I considered to be a generous supply of linens, pots, pans, and dishes. A prized set of square shaped Melmac dishes and a television lamp had travelled well.

Our small Crosley television had also made the cross-country trip, only to find there was no over-the-air television signal in Flagstaff at the time. In a tender mercy, Flagstaff's cable television system would become available to Cottage City residents in a few months.

The dim images produced on the black and white television screens were better viewed with the major lights turned off, so television lamps adorned the top of almost all television sets across the country. Our television lamp may have been our most lovely possession, spiraling white glass with a substantial number of multicolored marbles embedded in it.

With the arrival of cable television in Cottage City, you could tell who was at home by noting the soft and changing light of the television set radiating through the windows of an otherwise darkened living room.

This was a time when television actually created a warm and rather intimate environment, regularly encouraging conversations and, at times, even romance. Since it would have been necessary to get up from the couch to change the channel on your set, you would stay closely seated through the commercials, talking to one another.

This is an intimacy now lost in the illuminating glare of the massive high definition screens that command our attention in a fully lit room as we maintain a death grip on our remote controls.

At times, there was music provided courtesy of Lucky Strike cigarettes, the sponsor of <u>Your Hit Parade</u> with its countdown for the week's top ten songs.

The light reflecting through the diversity of colored marbles embedded in our television lamp gave our unit a distinctive and attractive glow. I was proud of it, and Billie loved it. This television lamp, a wedding gift acquired from Cheek's Jewelry in Sallisaw, Oklahoma, was Billie's unqualified favorite piece of furniture.

Cottage City was on the southern most edge of the property bounded by the campus on the north and by grassy meadows to the south. When spring and wild flowers came, it was beautiful, but in quite a different manner from the lush river bottom meadows of eastern Oklahoma. Nonetheless, the landscape gave the illusion of a grassy expanse dotted with the occasional pine tree as it moved toward the Naval Observatory sitting just to the southeast of Cottage City.

It was the climate, the cold windy weather, and the significant snowfalls that provided the greatest surprises. A two to four inch snowfall that would have lingered on the ground for days in Oklahoma would be gone by mid-afternoon. The moisture quickly absorbed into the volcanic base upon which Flagstaff seemed to have been placed.

Cooking was especially different. The nearly seven thousand foot altitude of Flagstaff demanded adjustments to even the most basic of recipes. Crispy and crunchy beans were avoided by soaking them at least twenty-four hours before cooking, instant potatoes became preferred over the real things and the baking of cakes required an adjustment, the complexities of which remain a puzzlement to me.

We were strangers in an anomalous and unfamiliar place, but we were committed to stay a bit.

Not having a vehicle, the proximity of essential services had to be addressed.

Early on, it appeared to us that the closest grocery was a Safeway located near the junction of Highway 89 and U.S. 66. It was physically close, but a sizeable chain link fence separated the store from the campus. For the first month or so, our next door neighbors to the west, Sally and Alfred Hicks, offered to watch David while we would make our way to the grocery, following a path that required us to climb the fence behind the Science Building. Upon our return trip, I would boost Billie up and she would climb over first; I would then stand on a rock outcropping and pass the grocery bags across the fence. The exchange completed, I would climb over and we would continue our walk home.

Through visits with other wives, Billie discovered Foodtown, a locally owned grocery, slightly further from our door than the Safeway but without the inconvenience of the formidable fence. The store was patronized by locals and the merchandise was considerably better priced.

In his stroller, David could now make the trip.

The beef was good. The produce was acceptable Flagstaff quality, not a particularly high bar to clear. Along the store's south wall, respectably removed from the entry path, was a large selection of beer. The novelty alone made it intriguing. With Oklahoma still deeply entrenched in the philosophy of prohibition, beer was not a part of the standard grocery store inventory in Stigler.

Although I was underage, this became our grocery shopping ritual. I would stop at the beer section and select a quart of beer for purchase. Coors, a brand not then available in Oklahoma, was the popular choice for placement in our cart.

Billie would offer no objection. We then worked our way through the aisles, Billie carefully selecting the essentials to get us to the next pay check. I would cautiously total the cost of the groceries in our basket. We would arrive at a point that I would say, "We can afford it if I put the beer back." She would agree, and I would return the quart of beer to its place on the shelf.

Similarly, I suspect Billie's thoughts of Coca-Cola were sublimated into the purchase of Kool-Aid packages. Still, even then, a chilled pitcher of sweet tea could be found in our refrigerator.

While my quart of beer would gradually make its way closer and closer to the checkout stand, it would be a considerable time before the first quart of beer would travel from the shelves of Foodtown into our refrigerator.

During a recent shopping trip to Whole Foods, Billie discovered cupcakes filled with Peanut Butter and Jelly and a package of star-shaped gummy bears had oddly made their way into our basket.

When asked, I answered, "Whole Foods only sells healthy, organic stuff. I'm sure these are good for me."

Perhaps some things don't change over time if you are willing to accept the hypothesis that the coveted beer of my youth has been mystically transformed through the passage of time into cupcakes and gummy bears.

I was directed to a barber shop located across the street from Foodtown where an ASC student had a chair. He had gone to barber college to have a stable method of paying for his education. While not Walter Lewis, he was a good barber.

Next door to the barber shop was the Spudnut Shop. The scent of the doughnuts and cinnamon rolls hinted at another unaffordable temptation. There are few smells the equal of the aroma of fresh doughnuts.

Billie and the Boys

Once we had made the decision to come to Arizona State, we had managed to save a reasonable amount of money during our remaining months in Stigler. While the hospital bills for David's birth used up some of our savings, Grandmother and Granddaddy McBride, along with Mother and Dad, paid the lion's share of the bill. My scholarship provided us with campus housing, utilities included, and $50 a month. So while our finances were not yet at critical mass, caution had to be exercised. It was important for Billie to find some type of job.

Within the month, Billie was directed to a job selling tickets at the Orpheum Theatre. Although television was taking its toll on the movie business elsewhere, in Flagstaff the Orpheum, with its downtown location, was continuing to thrive. It was the only theatre in a college town.

As I recall, Billie made 65 cents an hour with the perk of a bag or two of unsold popcorn most nights and, on occasion, unsold hot dogs.

I would bundle David up each night she worked, and we would walk to the theatre. Most evenings, I would push him in the stroller. On snowy nights, I carried him. David and I saw the endings of a lot of movies.

As soon as the second showing had begun, Billie would reconcile her cash drawer and was ready to go home. A large sack of surplus popcorn frequently accompanied us.

During January and February of 1958, we would walk directly home. While we brought the warmest clothing we owned, it was no match for Flagstaff's winter nights. I was grateful someone had been far-sighted enough to buy David an unbelievably warm snow suit. Without that snow suit, the walks might not have been possible. I believe we all enjoyed the walks. I found them to be splendid fun.

When we were fortunate enough to get a more moderate night, we'd walk around the corner for a bout of window shopping at Sears, J.C. Penny and Babbitt's. Now we were mostly window shopping appliances and furniture.

Most nights, we would come into our home and stand next to the vented heating stove to warm our hands. Billie's hands, then as now, were beautiful. Her long graceful fingers moved as if she was trying to capture the heat. It was a pleasant and reassuring ritual that warmed both hands and heart.

Then, with David tucked in, we would sit on the twin bed/couch, eat the popcorn, and share our days.

We talked and laughed and spoke of our tomorrows.

A belief in the potential of tomorrows should never lose its allure.

I still like walks in the snow. I must acknowledge walks through the Oklahoma ice and snow are now strongly influenced by the demands of my Cairn terrier, littleman.

Regardless, it was Billie's theatre income that absolutely made the difference for us during those early months.

As our budget allowed, we explored the great culinary variety of Flagstaff. At first, it was limited to the free or nearly free. The free included an introduction to pizza at a bar and grill near campus operated by a Chinese family. The owner's brother, Jersey Woo, was a student at ASC and was seemingly often around basketball practices. On occasion, at his brother's establishment, Jersey would make us the pizza of our choice and draw us a glass of beer. We discovered green chili pizza. Ethnically, it was a little Italian, a little Mexican, and a lot Chinese. It was very tasty.

It wasn't long until Billie brought a box of Appian Way Pizza Mix home from Foodtown. She made a pizza of cheese, browned hamburger meat, and green chilies. Billie's creation was a little Italian, a little Mexican, and a lot Okie. I still find satisfaction in the thought of nice slice of Okie pizza.

During these early days in Flagstaff, I was learning Okie was an ethnic group, along with Black, Mexican, Indian, Chinese, and so on. So, a little Okie food seemed to fit right into Flagstaff's variety of cultural cuisine. The Flagstaff of 1958 was quite culturally diverse. While perhaps not altogether tolerant, it was nonetheless varied.

The smells pouring out of the Mexican food restaurants were enticing, but for a while we would just smell. We would hear rave reviews of the El Charro not far from the campus on South San

Billie and the Boys

Francisco Street. We discovered green chile burritos and chile rellenos at the El Charro.

It was Billie's cooking and her skill to "make do" that was unparalleled. She said, "As long as I can get milk, eggs, and flour, I can feed us."

She baked pies that brought the neighbors from several units around us to our front door. The walls were thin. Yes, there was lard in the crust. Her pie crusts were magnificent. Gratefully, it would be a number of years before we had to discover pie wasn't one of the basic food groups.

High altitude cake recipes, the extended time required to prepare regular potatoes forcing her to yield to instant potatoes, and beans having to be soaked for extensive periods of time prior to cooking were all adjustments that Billie made quickly. "Even water boils differently at 7000 feet."

I repeatedly attempted to prepare a meal. It was usually spam baked with a slice of pineapple on top or cheeseburger steaks.

My intentions were always better than my meals.

CHAPTER TWO

Student Athletes

It is not my intent to completely ignore my athletic experience in Flagstaff. A basketball scholarship was the enticement that brought us to Arizona. It was a positive experience of which I remain both proud and pleased. I simply do not want to write anything that resembles the telling of "old war stories" of competitions played out over 50 years ago. It was the relationships with my teammates that I enjoyed and continue to value.

I believe everyone remembers their jersey numbers. At Stigler High School, I was twenty-four and at Arizona State, I was six.

Ira Andrews, a Tucson native, was the first to approach me. We were on the floor shooting well before anyone else arrived, and Ira was just Ira. Ira was a truly fine point guard and a reliable friend.

Sophomores Bill Aaron and Wiley Horton are now members of the Northern Arizona University Hall of Fame.

Senior Wayne McGrath would eventually become President of Eastern Arizona Community College in Thatcher, Arizona. I do not know what became of Senior John Hight. I know that to this day, his sixty seven points is the second highest single game total ever scored by an Arizona high school player. It is my suspicion that he was as solid a citizen as he was a solid player.

Bobby Olivas was the most competitive and intense teammate I ever had at any level or in any sport. I suspect Bobby is unchanged.

Kent Briggs from Phoenix was clearly the kindest person and finest young man on the team. Conversations with Kent put my recollections of Mema Lane's rudimentary musings on Mormonism into a more substantial contextual format.

Human Anatomy, a class required of all Physical Education and Science majors, helped me find even more of a niche.

The material was difficult and the instructor was unyielding. This class was considered by both groups to be the "wash-out class."

I have always believed I learned more in intricate classes taught by demanding instructors than in any other classroom. I believe this remains true for every serious student on most university campuses. If this logic is flawed then I have unduly contributed to the intellectual discomfort of a number of students over the years.

While certain previous professors had made minor allowances for the PE majors, Marjorie Glendening was not so inclined. She was an excellent teacher with a superb grasp of the material. She measured every student within the framework of her very high standards. Her examinations required both rote memory and a creative application of the knowledge.

Her grading was severe. I would later serve as her lab assistant for a semester, and I came to understand she determined a student's grade based upon a comparative structure that contained every student who had ever taken her class, not just those who might be in a given class during a given semester. She considered the assignment of an unworthy grade as diminishing every grade she had ever assigned to any student.

So, an A was an A, and she distributed very few of them. C was the most commonly occurring grade, an outcome which led many students to seek a major outside the science area. D's were not gifts, they were well-earned grades. Many a student proudly walked across that graduation stage and exited ASC with a D in Human Anatomy adorning their transcript.

Dr. Glendening graded with an integrity and wisdom I rarely encountered over my years in education. No grade was assigned capriciously.

I am certain that today, someone would market a tee shirt saying "I survived Glendening's Anatomy!"

Entering the lecture hall over which Ms. Glendening presided for the first time, I spotted one of my basketball team mates, Randy Randolph, seated in the back row along with several football players. I recognized Hosie Maddox and Bill McCormick. Without invitation, I joined them in the rear of the room.

Over the next few weeks through labs and lectures, I suspected almost the entire group was struggling both with the volume of material with the brisk nature of its presentation. Shortly after the first exam was returned, the head football coach, Max Spilsbury, came into the locker room after a basketball practice and asked me to stop in his office before I left. I did.

I waited as he completed something or the other. Then, he told me several of the guys had come to him about Anatomy and that he had spoken with Ms. Glendening.

"She said you were the only athlete who even resembled a student, told me I should maybe get you to tutor them because she wasn't going to do it."

He offered to pay me for my services. I said I would but declined the money. I had been on campus barely a month and it just seemed like bad policy to me. I knew I couldn't take the test for them.

Coach and I agreed on a night for them to come to the unit. I know I felt a bit awkward going into the class the next day. When Hosie grabbed my shoulders from behind and gave me a healthy "Thanks!" my concerns dissipated.

I told Billie that three or four of the guys would be coming to study and let it go at that. I should have a little more descriptive of Hosie.

I should have told her he was a mountain of young man. I should have told her he was going to fill the entire doorway with his physical presence. I should have told her Hosie was as black as the mountain after midnight. You know, I just didn't think about it.

Billie and the Boys

Hosie and Randy arrived first. I was rocking David, so Billie went to the door. She opened the door, then recoiled a full two yards into the room.

Realizing he had startled her, Hosie was delighted; his incredible smile filled his face. Randy just hooted. I'm sure there were some Okie comments made. There often were.

Over fifty years have now passed, years in which I have rarely seen Billie retreat, and I can still visualize Hosie framed in our doorway as Billie took her big hop back into the room.

In the room, Hosie came directly to me and extended his hands for David. Given the enhancements of time and memory, it seems his hands were so large that he just cradled David in his palm. David just melted in his hands.

By evening's end, it was Billie that Hosie figuratively had in the palm of his hand, a fact that likely saved me from considerable chastisement for not having better prepared her for his arrival.

Of all the people I considered my friends, Hosie was Billie's favorite.

Hosie, Randy, Bill McCormick, and I met weekly. Everyone passed Human Anatomy. For the duration of our time on campus, we remained fast friends.

I don't want to give the illusion there was not racial tension on the Arizona State campus in 1958, because there was. I recall one day between classes, Ira Andrews and I were sitting in the Student Union, just visiting and drinking coffee.

Some forgettable soul asked me, "You just hang out with colored guys?"

I was startled; the question stumped me and I must have stammered.

Ira, never being one to lack for words, responded for me. "Who else gonna' hang out with an Okie?"

He smiled and his contagious laugh escaped him. I laughed. I remember the folks in the booth behind us started laughing. I don't remember the guy who inquired. He just melted away.

It was funny then, and it is funny now. It was sad then, and it is sad now.

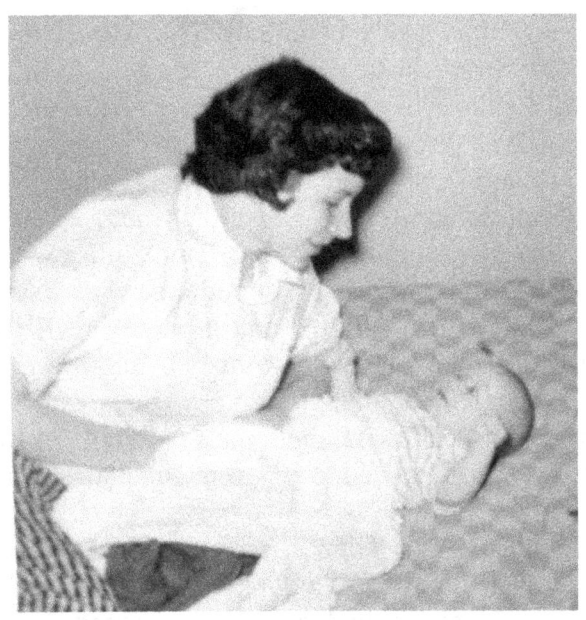

CHAPTER THREE

Cottage City 1958

Living in the unit to the east of ours was Dean and Jody Resuis, from Buffalo Center and Pella, Iowa, respectfully. Jody was a fine athlete, and Dean was as genuinely interested in education as any individual I would encounter.

Dean sat and played cards with me the day of my grandfather's funeral. While this might have been a random act of kindness for Dean, it was more meaningful for me.

They would leave at the end of the first summer session, returning to southern Minnesota. I wish we could have known them longer.

When they left, they sold us a room divider that Dean had built. It was constructed of heavy plywood, triple hinged, with three folding sections. We proudly placed the divider between the couch and stove, shielding the kitchen from view and giving a sense of boundary to the living room. We were delighted with the divider.

Billie and the Boys

A Navajo couple, Alfred and Sally Hicks, lived in the unit to the west. They were distant until we engaged them. They had been reared on the Navajo Reservation, and their families still lived there. They often communicated with each other in the Navajo language regardless of the presence of others. There were profound social differences, so unlike the Cherokee and Choctaw friends we had grown up with in Stigler and Sallisaw.

It brought to mind what my grandfather had told me about coming to Stigler in the 1920's and promptly realizing that he needed to learn some Choctaw words. He felt you had to learn enough of your neighbor's language to say hello, goodbye, and to inquire as to their health and about their children. So I learned to do that in Navajo. I wish I could remember the words Alfred taught me.

Connie and Lamar Haines, slightly older than us, lived behind us and one unit over. They were just enough older that we came to find their counsel both credible and sound.

Lamar was the Wilson Sporting Goods representative for several states, but in an effort to save the money toward the purchase of a home, they were taking advantage of college housing while Connie finished her degree. Although they had two small children, Vickie and Lee, they found room under their wings for us.

Lamar was well known throughout northern Arizona. He maintained an office in Tissaws, a local sporting goods store. He was an enthusiastic hunter and fine camp cook.

He was born and raised on a ranch near Winkelman, a small community to the south of Globe. This was an area of desert and arid mountains, spotted with saguaro cactus and punctuated by slot canyons which often contained unexpected clear mountain streams on their floor.

Having come to Flagstaff for college and football in 1948, there was nothing this native son of Arizona did not love about her northern mountains.

Why he repetitively invited me, such a comparative neophyte, into the woods with him, I never really understood, but I am grateful he did. We would walk miles into the wilderness, rarely speaking other than through hand gestures. Lamar detested those who hunted from a stand. "You can't really get to where the deer live. Got to walk with'em."

Lamar literally could track a deer over relatively rocky terrain.

Hunting in the junipers was different from hunting in the pines and aspens. Lamar considered hunting at 6000 feet hunting downhill and hunting from 8000 feet to the tree line hunting uphill. He hunted every location differently.

"If you look, a place will tell how it wants to be hunted."

"Always follow the game trails. They know where they're going. We don't."

From Mormon Lake to Kendrick Peak to the tree line of Humphrey's Peak to outcroppings on the Mogollon Rim, Lamar gave me his personal tour of the Coconino National Forest. There might be outdoor experiences the equal of sitting on the edge of the Mogollon eating Vienna sausage, pork and beans, and jerky procured from the reservation, but there are none better.

Always leaving well before sunrise, Lamar would drive his old truck to a site he had preselected. It seemed to me that he knew every mountain, every hill, and every slot canyon in the forests of northern Arizona. Yet, he seemed to always hold the belief that he would see something new. He hoped for a sight he hadn't seen before, for a game trail that promised to lead him to a place in the wilderness he hadn't already been. So much of northern Arizona was still genuine wilderness.

Lamar and Connie would leave Cottage City and purchase a small stone house on North Beaver Street near the hospital. We remained close until Lamar's death in 1986.

Living directly behind us were Bob and Mary Ellen Vega with their son, John. Bob had played minor league baseball out of high school and, as with most, it didn't work out well for him. Sports had been a major portion of his identity, so he now had to find his way into a life with which he was unfamiliar. Mary Ellen, a pretty girl who was sustaining her "baby weight," was bright, possessing a balancing sense of herself coupled with a genuine wit.

We hardly knew her when early one morning, she came bouncing in with her fuzzy house shoes flopping and John on her hip, for coffee and a visit. She proclaimed to Billie, "Told Bob he could either have a little or have breakfast." She paused for dramatic effect and continued, "He went to class hungry!"

Bob and Mary Ellen were the neighbors that provided the comic relief. Bob was the perfect "Desi" to Mary Ellen's "Lucy." When the walls are paper thin and baths and kitchens abut, life flows more amiably if you have adjacent neighbors with a sizeable sense of humor.

Spring and summer come late in Flagstaff, but they are well worth the wait. It was not the smothering humidity of an eastern Oklahoma evening where imperfect relief could be found in the breeze of oscillating fans while laying on sprinkled sheets.

On spring nights, bedroom windows were opened, allowing a fresh, pleasant, pine scented breeze to fill our bedroom. David's crib was against an interior wall and only feet away. Our bed was but a walk space from the windows. We would awaken, snuggling in the cool of the Flagstaff morning, before daybreak. We spoke delicately so as not to stir our sleeping son, speaking of the coming day and of our days to come.

Billie's morning hair was so curly and black; her eyes a poignant blue.

The memories of Flagstaff mornings remain a tonic for my soul.

CHAPTER FOUR

The Weatherford Hotel

My first job was at the Mount Elden Drive-In Theatre in East Flagstaff. For four or five hours each evening, I would secure the money as a car would arrive, carry the money to a cashier, and then return with a ticket to be placed on the dash by the customer. Later, I would walk the lot until the feature ended, and then I would stand with a flashlight directing traffic from the theatre. I think I was able to get this job because the owners were so pleased with Billie.

I had only been at the theatre a few weeks when my real employment break came in late April of 1958. The lab instructor in my anatomy class, Jim is the only name I recall, was working at the Weatherford Hotel as the desk clerk on the evening shift. The student who had been working the 11-7 was leaving Flagstaff and going to the valley to complete the final portion of his

Billie and the Boys

student teaching. The 11-7 shift was open, and Jim recommended me.

I had an interview with Ann Hall, the owner of the hotel. Her husband had bought the hotel, dreamed great dreams and died, leaving the operation of the hotel to his widow.

I got the position with the starting pay of $1.00 an hour, in large measure because of Jim's endorsement. I believe this was the most excited I had been about getting a job since my grandfather hired me at Hays and Buchanan when I was twelve.

I kept both jobs until early August, saving all the drive-in money to put toward a car before winter returned. During the summer of 1958, I worked at the drive-in from 5 pm to about 10 pm, at the Weatherford from 11pm to 7am, had summer classes from 7:40 am to 10:50, went home to eat and rest and went to the gym from 3:30 to 4:30, and started all over again. Sunday night was my night off at the hotel. Some schedules you do not ever forget. I know I was glad when summer session ended in July.

Sally Hicks, our next door neighbor to the west, began to baby-sit David during the periods when Billie or I was not available to keep him. While each stay was relatively brief, the arrangement persisted over a length of time. David really seemed to enjoy Sally, who would play with him and her son on the floor and sing traditional Navajo songs.

When David began talking, his early conversations consisted of crisp and understandable words followed by garble. But the verbalizations were consistent. We begin to consider the possibility of a speech issue.

We considered it until I came in from class one winter morning and sat down to have a cup of coffee with Sally and Alfred before taking David next door. David had gotten up in my lap. Sally was talking to him, speaking in Navajo, and David clearly understood. David's speech difficulty was that he was speaking a blend of English and Navajo. We were pleased and relieved.

I had no concept of the substantial history of the Weatherford Hotel. I knew the hotel existed because only an alley separated it from the Orpheum Theatre and there was a fine little hot dog stand just off the alley that covered their dogs with generous portions of relish. Over the next few years, I would come to know and appreciate the history and the folklore of the hotel.

As with most downtown hotels in the late 1950's, The Weatherford was trying to survive. A surging motel business located directly on Route 66 increasingly captured those traveling by automobile. They offered parking with direct access to your room, modern conveniences, and brilliant flashing neon signs. There is no question the ribbon of motels and restaurants along the north side of Route 66 was seductive to the growing population now traveling by automobile.

A few of the motels had swimming pools. The standing joke among Flagstaff folks was that these attractive but unheated pools were usable for about three hours on one day in early August, but no one was certain which day that might be. Families were attracted to the motels while some adult travelers, in part to avoid proximity to railroad tracks, were attracted to the Weatherford or its main downtown competitor, the Monte Vista.

Like the station wagons and finely finned Detroit produced automobiles their customers drove, these business were "new and shiny," appealing to the new, more mobile lifestyle of a now vacationing America.

The Weatherford Hotel, a sturdy stone testimonial to travel in the first half of the twentieth century, sat on the southwest corner of Leroux and Aspen. Constructed with large blocks of stone, it reflected the concepts of permanence and durability valued in an era when cross-country travel was primarily by rail and powered by brawny and durable locomotives. In so many ways, Flagstaff stood with a foot firmly planted in both halves of the twentieth century. Route 66 was now lined on the north by vivid neon signs announcing motels and restaurants and on the south by multiple railroad tracks leading into the brick passenger station in downtown Flagstaff.

The automobile was changing the manner in which Americans traveled as well as our expectations concerning the durability of the automobiles we drove. Now it seems to have also reflected a changing relationship with permanence.

Billie and the Boys

The hotel was opened by Flagstaff pioneer, John Weatherford, on January 1, 1900. It had served the community well during its first 50 years. By 1958, with less than half of the rooms having a private bath, the Weatherford prospered during the summer months and struggled to survive during the balance of the year.

Then as now, the Grand Canyon was the area's most recognized attraction. Zane Grey fans came to Weatherford to stay in the room where this storied western author had often taken temporary residence and is said to have written several of his works. Many of these fans were authors themselves in search of vicarious inspiration.

The Weatherford's preeminent local external asset was its proximity to the railroad station and the bus depot. A contract with Greyhound and with Greyline Tours provided a steady stream of tourists traveling by bus to visit the Grand Canyon. So, as it was with Flagstaff's tourist based business community, you made your money in the summer and hung on the rest of the year.

It strikes me that the Weatherford Hotel of 1958 is not far removed from where I now find myself at this time of my life. I am standing with one foot in the last two-thirds of the 20th Century and tentatively sticking my toes into the 21st Century, checking the temperature of an emerging, evolving culture that is enamored by speed, technology, and disposability; a culture that assigns the same credibility to the musing of cynical television comedians as to the thoughts found in a New York Times Opinion Editorial.

I find a sense of permanence, a feeling of belonging, to be attractive. I am most comfortable when I can read and absorb contradictory information before committing fully to a position. Wedged in my logic is the concept that there is a difference in the rapid development of information and actually understanding how to reasonably apply the newly generated knowledge.

I suppose I view it as I look upon eating your food too fast. Effective digestion is impaired and you cannot articulate your thoughts when your mouth is full. I am not even certain you can think and chew at the same time.

It seems an inefficient technique that in the end produces an excessive amount of waste.

Such ramblings aside, the night shift was available and I took it.

The night shift afforded me an opportunity to learn the procedures of the front desk without the concentrated volume of check-ins that the evening shift routinely managed with the arrival of groups touring by Greyhound. There were just a few stragglers registering during the night shift. Arrivals on an eleven o'clock bus from Phoenix or travelers who had driven later on Route 66. The latter group was seeking a place to sleep a few hours and expected a bargain rate. There were no bargain rooms to be found in Flagstaff during the summer months. I was alone at the desk telling a weary traveler that there was no deal to be made for maybe a remaining room or explaining that the sign saying there was no vacancy actually meant there was no vacancy.

Come the winter months, there would be vacancies and I would have the latitude to negotiate the price. The Weatherford policy on summer room rates was firm.

Hotel guests registered at a relatively small desk area. Individual sign-in cards, once completed, were placed in a slotted rack behind the room number and covering the red card that indicated a vacant room. The switchboard was a plug-in board with a main line into the hotel and four rollover lines. The desk clerk was also the hotel telephone operator.

Wake-up calls were set on a clock that had pegs at fifteen minute intervals. Properly set, the clock would ring at the selected time until it was manually turned off. Most mornings, the wake-up calls would begin about 4:30 AM.

"Good Morning, this is your 4:30 wake up call."

During the summer months, the hotel was full almost every night. The rooms without a private bath were considered inconvenient only by the American guests. Canadian guests seemed accepting and accommodating. European travelers, the majority of whom were French or English, considered such arrangements to be the norm and on occasion actually expressed their pleasure at the number of common baths to each floor. All

Billie and the Boys

knew the status of the bath situation when they booked a tour. There was no elevator to help guests who were going to stay on the second floor.

There was a bellhop on duty during the busy morning and evening times to assist with the luggage. Although the bellhop sat just across from the desk and in a direct line with the front door, I was provided with a bell to ring in case I could not find him.

The most frequent bellhops on duty seemed to be a tall, slender, and obsessively neat Mexican high school student named Victor and the short, muscular Edward who was in perpetual pursuit of a mustache that always seemed to be just escaping him. Both worked primarily for tips.

Edward was the hawk. He did an excellent job from the time he saw a suitcase near the front door. I believe he did very well with his tips during the summer. I remember him well because at times, he reminded me of Bill Grubbs who would hawk the front door of the men's side of Hays and Buchanan in Stigler.

I came to realize the seemingly useless front desk bell was at times required to summon Edward back to the lobby. He was prone to dally after escorting a young lady he judged to be particularly attractive to her room.

Victor, on the other hand, was more dependable and determined, always on time, always in a white shirt, and never grousing to leave early on a slow evening.

The only television in the building was located in the lobby. It was rare for anyone to be watching television after the 9 PM shows concluded; the 10 o'clock news had not yet a cultural fixture. The television was a source of entertainment. Newspapers and magazines were the source of detailed and credible information. The couches were arranged to form a conversation area with the television located along the north wall, appearing to be almost an afterthought.

It was not unusual to have a guest request a wake-up call when the morning newspapers arrived. Guests would appear at the base of the staircase and make their way to the desk in the most interesting garb to secure an *Arizona Republic*. Women would pause to survey the lobby before proceeding while men simply charged directly toward the newspapers stacked on the desk near the switchboard.

On most shifts between the hours of midnight and the 4:30, I would study, read for pleasure, or carefully deliberate over the maps provided by the U.S. Forest Service. I learned the geography and topography of Northern Arizona with the Grand Canyon, and the Navajo and Hopi Reservations from pouring over those maps. Within a month I could intelligently discuss the attractions of the region with an inquiring guest.

It would be a considerable time before Billie and I would actually go to the Grand Canyon.

I know my desire to familiarize myself with the state and the area came, in part, from an error in pronunciation I made in the first week of a required speech class. It was one part of an obligatory introduction assignment in which we were to introduce a classmate to the other members of the class. The student I was to introduce was from Ajo, which, to the delight of a classroom filled with Arizona natives, I proceeded to pronounce as "A-Joe" rather than the correct "Ah-hoe".

With that experience in mind, on slow winter evenings I solicited Edward and Victor to help with my Spanish enunciation. Upon his arrival in Stigler, my grandfather had made every effort to learn a few Choctaw words, feeling that if you were to live in a man's country you should learn a bit of his language. Similarly, I worked at learning a bit of Spanish.

Still, mostly, alone during the night, I read and poured over maps in the quiet.

In Flagstaff, the Independence Day holiday meant Pow-Wow came to town. I had just settled into my night shift job when Pow-Wow arrived and I learned of its raucous nature. Navajos, Hopis, and contingents from other smaller tribes poured into Flagstaff for this annual gathering. I wasn't prepared for the arrival of families in rubber wheeled wagons pulled by donkey or by horse.

There were parades every morning; the performances of the dancers during these parades were colorful, jaw-dropping sights for me. Billie and I loved the Pow-Wow parades.

Billie and the Boys

Early in the morning of July 5, 1958, I heard police sirens. Momentarily, the sound of a motorcycle roared into earshot. The cyclist flew down the sidewalk, passing only feet from the entrance to the Weatherford. With a quick turn, bike and rider shot past the light pole toward Spouse-Reitz, the dime store catty-corner from the Weatherford. He proceeded full throttle toward the dime store, then hoisted the bike up onto its rear wheel and maneuvered it around the pole before heading across the street to the west.

I moved to the front door of the Weatherford for a better view of the events.

The police car was now in the center of the intersection. The cyclist rounded a light pole, seemingly determined to ride a cloverleaf around all four lights. He flew directly past the policeman who stood by his vehicle with extended arms as if somehow intent upon catching the cyclist as he blew past. I can still see the policeman unsuccessfully waving his arms in the center of the street as the weaving rider flashed by him. Now, so many years later, it has become a "Barney Fife Moment."

Two more police cars arrived. The cyclist tried to complete his circle around the light pole, but he laid the bike over, sending him spilling on to the pavement. The cyclist lay on his back laughing, not a mocking laugh, but one of simple, shameless pleasure. There was naïve innocence in his laugh. The Flagstaff Police rushed to the arrest.

What impressed me then and continues to impress me today in light of our nation's history since 1958 was the kindness with which the Flagstaff Police assisted this visibly intoxicated young man to his feet. I vividly recall one officer dusting off the boy's clothes and giving a quick cursory check for injury before handcuffing him.

There would be multiple arrests over the course of a Pow-Wow ranging from public intoxication to disturbing the peace to indecent exposure, most of the latter occurring due to a shortage of restrooms and showers in the city park camp area or around the fair grounds.

The "prisoners" were taken to a make-shift fenced stockade at the park to be held overnight, then fed and released come morning.

My telling of the story the next day seemed to simply draw a "that's Pow-Wow" response from my neighbors, all of whom were more familiar with the Pow-Wow experience.

I remember Pow-Wow as colorful and entertaining while bringing a seemingly pure and meaningful joy to its participants.

When summer sessions at ASC ended in late July, Jim, who worked the three to eleven shift and had helped me get the job at the Weatherford, graduated and left. I was given the three to eleven shift, and I was thrilled to have it. It was close enough to the retail business I had grown up around that I enjoyed the front desk.

A Cottage City neighbor who was rapidly becoming a very close friend, Paul Lansing, took the night shift job.

While on the night shift, I had rarely seen the owner, Ann Hall, although she lived in an apartment on the ground floor of the hotel. Now, I would see her many work days. Before five, she was an astute businesswoman who asked good questions and gave good advice on tour arrivals and patron management. At five, she left her second floor office and retired to her quarters.

She would reappear after nine, framed in the half-light of the hallway, unsteady on her feet and with one of her many long flowing robes draped over her in a manner that did not always cover the essentials. Unexpectedly emerging from the brownish yellow light of the parallel hallway leading to her apartment, she startled more than one tourist on their way to a first floor room. And that first night, she startled her new evening shift desk clerk.

The after nine o'clock directives she gave were clumsily articulated and contradictory to the logic of her earlier conservations. She was the paradox that emerges when common sense becomes infused with alcohol.

I am sure during my first encounter with this ambiguity, I looked rather bewildered. Edward and Victor, more familiar with Mrs. Hall's nocturnal ramblings, had a chuckle at my expense and then told me it was a regular and common occurrence.

Victor explained, "She just gets liquored up to keep away the dark."

It was the first time I had heard the term "liquored up," and I found it to be quite descriptive of the condition.

As life has worn on, the phrase has taken on a more personal meaning as I have found several of those to whom I was close and who I loved also begin to drink enough to keep the darkness away. These were wastes that still touch points of deep sadness.

Victor or Edward, at times both, would assist her back to her apartment. If she became really insistent about it, they would escort her up to the office.

Promptly learning she had little or no recall of her late evening ramblings, all drunken directives were henceforth ignored. This was knowledge that everyone on the Weatherford staff except me already possessed.

I keep the expression "liquored up to keep the dark away" wedged tightly in my personal logic.

CHAPTER FIVE

Summer Guests

James, my brother, was our first arrival. We concluded he had been somewhat exiled by Mother and Dad. It was our first hint that my folks desired to put a little distance between James and his girlfriend, Wilma.

He slept on the twin bed, got a decent job at a service station on Route 66 and worked about two weeks. We awoke one morning to a note that he had left to return to Stigler.

Flagstaff was on the most direct route from Sallisaw to Las Vegas. Although they did not stay in our unit, Billie's sister, Lou, and her husband, Charles stayed the night in Flagstaff several times during our years there.

On their way to Las Vegas, they would drive through Flagstaff at all hours in a frantic rush to reach the dice tables in the desert. Win or lose, they would stop during their more leisurely return to Sallisaw.

Their first visit came in the mid summer of 1958. Lou and Billie went shopping. Lou put twenty-five percent down on a washer, a couch with something of a daybed, and a wicker bucket chair for us. Over the remaining Flagstaff years, I would joke with Billie that when Lou left after a visit, we always had a payment plan. I didn't really mind. Given Lou's family reputation, I'm not certain I would have complained anyway. I had heard the story of the Monopoly game.

As the story goes, Charles, Clayton Farmer, Boss Green and Barney Cheek were playing Monopoly in Charles' Ford dealership on a Sunday afternoon. Lou came to the door and found it locked. Seeing the men at a card table in the show room, she knocked.

Someone in the group thought it would be amusing to just ignore her. They did and she became increasingly insistent. Then

Clayton laughed, causing Charles to begin laughing. Lou Elba could get mad, high wide and handsome mad. The behavior of her husband and his friends did not sit well.

Lou selected a missile of convenience, a discarded brick. She stepped back and launched the brick though the plate glass window. As the shattered glass of the window finished falling, Lou lifted her dress and stepped into the showroom. Charles is said to have roared with laughter.

I have this fanciful mental image of my pretty, petite sister-in-law, maybe 17 years old at the time with her high heels and Sunday dress, stepping through the splintered plate glass window and striding into the showroom of her husband's Ford dealership.

Regardless, I never said a word about her assisted purchases other than, "Thank you very much."

Having a washing machine in our unit was a luxury that made our day to day life easier. Diapers and most clothing could be hung outside during the summer and dried on a rack over the heater in the winter. We only had to make occasional trips to the coin laundry at the end of our building to use the dryer.

Regardless, we had real couch, a real chair, our own washing machine, and a very real monthly payment.

Charles gave Billie a $100 dollar bill before he left.

Late one summer, Dad's youngest sister, Anna Lee, and her husband, Elic Cundiff, spent the night in Flagstaff. As I recall, Uncle Elic was a Major in the United States Army at the time and they were moving from one duty station to another.

Tired from the road, they nonetheless came by Cottage City before checking into their room at the Ramada Inn. Uncle Elic, slim and athletic, seeming to always exude a distinctive masculinity, exited the car smiling. He appeared absolutely unruffled by his travel. Auntie Ann, on the other hand, emerged seeming road-worn and snappy.

Uncle Elic, who always seemed to find a university campus invigorating, was enjoying sitting on our new couch and telling stories of his life on campus at Oklahoma A&M. Auntie's conversation was sufficiently crisp that it was obvious this was not a time she desired to visit. She unquestionably didn't want to hear my Uncle's entertaining tales nor did she want to respond to my inquiries about Mema Mac.

We arranged to meet at the Ramada for dinner and they left.

Several hours later, Billie and I arrived at the Ramada. Within minutes, a sparkling and vivacious Auntie Ann appeared. It was a jaw-dropping transformation. She was refreshed, elegantly dressed, and quite full of herself.

Anna Lee and Elic Cundiff were indeed a handsome couple.

Auntie was now brimming with stories from their last posting and looking forward to the next, I believe at Fort Benning, Georgia. But mostly, she told Stigler stories. The tale of the great ice cream theft and the story of the gravy knife Thanksgiving were ritually retold.

Although I knew the post office would no longer allow it, I reassured them it would not be necessary to send David an alligator from Georgia as they had sent to me. Nonetheless, knowing the creativity and commitment my uncle could bring to a whimsical mission, I tried to emphasis the point.

We ate, drank, and laughed. Aunt and Uncle had the knack of involving those surrounding them into their revelry with their warmth and gregariousness. We closed the restaurant. Uncle retrieved a bottle of Johnny Walker Red from their car and gave it to us. It was my first bottle of scotch whiskey, but not my last. We said goodbye. They departed before dawn. Though brief, their visit was a splendid reprieve.

After <u>To Bear Witness</u> was published, L. J. Davidson shared a recollection of Anna Lee with me. This writing brings it to mind.

To preface the story, L. J. had worked for my uncle, Hubert Claunts, at the Stigler 5 & Up as a boy. I was always told he got the job after pulling a drowning Tag Claunts from the Stigler swimming pool, a municipal pool located to the east of the water treatment plant below the dam at the old city lake.

It was L. J. who drove my mother in Uncle Hubert's car to Brentwood to spend Christmas with her parents in 1935. A few days later my parents eloped.

In the heart of the depression, the big bands reigned over popular music. Such bands played in the nightclubs that seemingly dotted eastern Oklahoma. A band of considerable reputation, the Stan Kenton orchestra by L. J.'s recollection, was playing in the area.

Not only was Anna Lee McBride stunningly beautiful, she was effervescent, flirtatious, and vibrantly filled with the energy of youth. Auntie Ann was considered to be the finest dancer as well as the finest dance partner in Stigler, Oklahoma.

It was the middle of an Oklahoma summer in the era prior to air conditioning; the young men were all dressed in their finest starched white shirts, and the young ladies were as lavishly dressed as a depression budget would allow. For this occasion, Auntie Ann chose to accent her dress with a cloth flower she had fashioned herself and dyed a brilliant red. She strategically placed the flower on her dress so as to further emphasize the existence of her cleavage.

The evening was hot and humid. There was substantial movement of young bodies and very little movement of air. The young men sweated while the young women glowed. Auntie Ann did not miss a single dance.

Many things went unnoticed in the heat and dim light of the tin roofed dance hall. As the evening came to an end and the lights were brought up, many a young man, L. J. confessing to be among them, could be seen wiping at a sizable red stain on the front of his white shirt.

With her red flower moist and fading, Anna Lee, reluctant to turn loose of the evening, remained radiantly transfixed in the center of the room. As she was prone to do, Auntie Ann left her mark.

As I said, Anna Lee and Elic Cundiff's visit was a grand reprieve.

CHAPTER SIX

Road Trips

In late May, we got a huge economic break when Billie was employed by Mountain States Telephone and Telegraph, the AT&T subsidiary for the Western United States. She got a highly coveted job as a telephone operator. The position provided good wages and great benefits, especially in a community with an abundant pool of inexpensive labor in the form of university students. I forget the exact wage, but I know it dramatically exceeded the amount I was making.

As well as money, it brought us a first-class perk: an affordable telephone. PRospect 4-3476 was installed at 85 Cottage City.

I cannot put into words how proud I was of my wife.

By mid-July, we had saved enough money for a down payment on a car. A steady shopping of the car lots of Flagstaff and discussions with friends suggested that Phoenix offered the most affordable automobiles.

So, on a cool Flagstaff Sunday morning in mid July, after I had finished my graveyard shift at the Weatherford, I walked the two blocks to the Greyhound Station, bought a one-way ticket and boarded the bus for Phoenix. I had never been to Phoenix beyond a road trip to Tempe aboard the Travel Jack, the ASC team bus, in February. Possessing a naïve confidence only youth can give, I was armed with directions provided by friends to two car lots on a stretch of Phoenix highway filled with used car dealers.

I had a map of the city I had cut from a larger map of Arizona and instructions concerning the Phoenix city bus system I had written with the obsessive-compulsive detail only concern about the unknown can produce. The two lots where former ASC

Billie and the Boys

athletes now worked were marked. I had called both men a day or so ahead and had been warmly received.

I slept for most of the early portion of the trip, but I got my first real glimpses of Sedona, Jerome, and Prescott. I fully awakened as the bus began its descent onto desert floor.

The Greyhound was not air-conditioned. The hot air flowing through the open windows got my attention. I was forced to consider the possibility that Phoenix in July might not resemble Tempe in February.

The bus arrived at the terminal a little before noon. I stepped from the water cooled terminal onto the blistering sidewalks of Phoenix. Any chamber of commerce hype concerning "a dry heat" was becoming completely unconvincing. Phoenix in July is hot!

My jeans begin to feel hot against my legs. It was a unique burning sensation.

The bus directions were immaculate. Car lot row was far larger than a similar concept cluster along 11th street in Tulsa. The first car lot had a large neon sign in the shape of a car that was most impressive. The man to whom I had spoken on the telephone was not working, but he had left a note for another salesman to show me what they had. I was unimpressed with the salesman and the inventory. I left a little disappointed and had some level of concern. But I had come to Phoenix to buy us a car.

The second lot was smaller with little of the glitz that decorated the majority of used car dealerships along the row. This man acted as if he was expecting me. We talked a little ASC football and basketball. Then, he took me to a light green and black, two door, six cylinder 1955 Plymouth with a standard shift as if he had been saving it for me.

Future experiences indicated he was candid about its liabilities and its assets. It was presented as possessing a good frame, good tires, solid transmission, and an oil leak. Importantly, Billie and I could afford it.

In a small building with its swamp cooler cranking, the deal was sealed. I rolled down all the windows on the car. As I began to drive, the Phoenix heat again impressed me. Again using my hand-crafted street map, I followed the arterial streets until I found my way back to the highway, Highway 69 as I recall, and began to make my drive back toward cooler air.

Following the directions Jim Wombacher, a new acquaintance and a follow Cottage City dweller reared in the Verde Valley, had mapped for me, I followed a route enabling me to avoid Prescott and Jerome by taking the completed sections of the new Black Canyon Highway to its contemporary end, then following a back road through Page Springs that would allow me to make my way into Sedona. From my seat on the Greyhound I had not really grasped the extent of the incline up the mountain. Over the next few hours, I would gain an entirely different definition for the words "steep" and "vertical."

Leaving the floor of the valley cradling Phoenix, it was the large saguaro cactus that first caught my eye. Beyond what I viewed as their impressive size, they all seemed to be signaling touchdown.

The afternoon was wearing thin, and I hoped to reach Sedona before dark. While over the coming years I would make many stops at Rock Springs for a lunch of burgers and pie or a breakfast of pancakes and eggs, this day I drove past the roadside café. I continued my steady climb north.

The descent into the Verde Valley was initially as disorientating as the views were spectacular. As the long incline from Phoenix softened and in the midst of a sweeping curve, the Verde Valley almost mystically spread out below me.

Although I now travel north on I-17, it is a sight I anticipate with great eagerness. Regardless of how often you might have peered over the edge into it, when the Verde Valley opens itself to you it spikes the imagination. I wonder what the early settlers might have felt at the sight of such a vista. Despite the passage of time, the sight remains visually captivating.

I made my way down into the valley. I decided not to stop in Camp Verde even though the downtown buildings crowded the road on both sides and the café in the old stagecoach station looked intriguing. I made an exit toward Cornville, taking the right turns on a road that was at times unpaved before ultimately arriving at the Page Springs Store.

Billie and the Boys

I remember the Page Springs Store as a slightly weathered frame building with a large porch and gas pumps out front. Trees draped over it in a willow like fashion. It adequately reminded me of the stores of rural eastern Oklahoma that it seemed a most comfortable place to stop. The interior with its sandwiches, some groceries, and a well-stocked Coke case seemed familiar. The Page Springs Store even smelled like the small country stores of Haskell County.

While not much of a river by Oklahoma measures, the Verde River flowed not far behind the store. It was not as large as the Barren Fork Creek as it moves toward its confluence with the Illinois River, but it was equally as clear. The sounds of the water were pleasing. I noted it for future return, but I took a pre-wrapped mystery meat sandwich and a bottle of Coca-Cola with me, eating as I continued my drive home.

The countryside appeared to make a flawless transition as I drove into Sedona, a small village that appeared to be mostly occupied by the farmers and ranchers who had been in the area for decades. Only the Matterhorn Motel built into the mountain side near the entry into Oak Creek Canyon hinted at its discovery by an increasing number of sight-seeing tourists.

Deeper into the canyon, Garland's Store looked as if it had been there since the canyon had be cut by the creek. It did not intrude upon the land.

I found Oak Creek to be incredibly inviting. The cars of late Sunday swimmers reluctant to leave dotted the shoulders of the road. Considering the crackling weather I left in Phoenix, a swim in the creek was tempting.

Driving at the slower speeds with the windows down allowed an auditory appreciation of Oak Creek Canyon that is fundamental to the experience. Even beyond the sounds, the smell of the water and the flora carried on cool canyon air filled the car. This seemed the most magical and intriguing place I had ever encountered. When you experience something like Oak Creek for the first time alone, there is an irrational fear it might never be this way again. I wished Billie was in the car.

On this return trip, ascending from the Phoenix furnace to the panorama of the Verde Valley, to a brief but very rejuvenating stop in the shade of Page Springs, through the indelible sounds of Oak Creek crashing through the steep walled canyon before suddenly rising from its floor by way of the switchbacks, finally emerging some 2000 feet above the Oak Creek floor into the dense pine forest near Flagstaff. On this drive, I started to grasp the vast openness and diversity of Arizona and how enthralled I was with its landscape. Northern Arizona felt so new and fresh. I was captivated.

I arrived home and for whatever reason one remembers such things; I remember Billie had cooked a beef roast and was waiting with dinner for me. Little is more welcoming than Billie and the smell of her beef roast.

Logic dictates we talked of the car first, but I could not wait to tell her about the places I had seen. Over dinner, I told her far more than she ever wanted to know about my drive home from Phoenix. She surely tired of my talk of Oak Creek Canyon.

I was happy to have a car that would make our life much easier. I could not wait to show Billie some of the places I felt I had discovered.

During the next few years, the 1955 Plymouth would teach me an invaluable lesson: I learned something can be flawed yet be absolutely ideal.

Not everything in your life has to be perfect to be perfect.

CHAPTER SEVEN

Oak Creek in August

Because of Billie's work schedule, our first drive in the newly acquired automobile came the next Sunday. We drove through the aspens and the pines to the Snow Bowl. We stopped in the empty parking lot not far from the lodge and looked west toward Kendrick Peak.

We retrieved the car seat we had brought with us from Stigler. It was the infant car seat of its time. It was a canvas bag with two holes for his legs suspended from a rubber covered metal frame that hooked over the front seat of the car. It gave him a great view. Fun it was, protective it wasn't.

I would say, "Put the boy in his bucket and we'll take a drive." And drive we did.

I insistently talked of the sights and sounds of Oak Creek with Billie, likely to the point of becoming rather annoying. I can do that. So before August was spent, we made our way down the switchbacks into Oak Creek Canyon.

The red rock formations were extraordinary, but it was the canyon floor with the creek rushing through the lush vegetation that really enthralled me. Places that excite you are best when shared.

Billie was impressed with the switchbacks, uncomfortable but impressed. As you completed the descent, the roof of the state trout farm became visible, and then the rushing creek seemed to just appear as if it had been released from somewhere deep inside the canyon wall.

Parking was creekside on the shoulder of 89A. You simply pulled over, got out, and walked down to the creek. There were no more than a couple of families at the place we randomly selected. The traffic was such that most people quite comfortably changed into swim suits in their cars.

When you shut off the motor, the sounds of the creek would fill the car with anticipation and exhilaration.

We had been told the water was chilly, but being told and actually feeling the chill is quite another story. The initial jolt of the cold water staggered us. Once settled into the creek, the experience met every expectation. Billie would sit on the rocks, allowing David to splash his feet in the water while I would sit shoulder deep in the languid pool.

We talked as I lounged in the water. Giving way to temptation and immaturity, I would occasionally splash water in the direction of Billie and David. The maneuver would elicit the familiar, "Don't you dare!"

We picnicked on a large flat boulder on the west side of the creek. Billie had prepared deviled eggs; she always prepared deviled eggs, and I never tired of them.

Formed of captured snow melt from the cradle of the San Francisco Peaks, Oak Creek emerges from the walls of the canyon as cold as the day it melted, as crystal clear as it was at the moment of its transformation from snow into water. The sounds the rushing water made as it hurried across the stones moving from pool to pool has the same sedative effect as the sound of waves. The canyon walls captured the sounds, causing them to reverberate across the canyon floor, seeming at once to come from downstream and upstream, depending upon where you were sitting.

All flowing streams make a comparable sound as water rushes over rocks; each is similar yet distinct.

The large, sun-baked boulders bordering the creek were as warm as the waters of the creek were cold. We lay upon a quilt carefully spread upon a boulder. In the canyon on an August afternoon, lying on a stone gazing up a vertical canyon wall into a brilliant blue Arizona sky with the sound of the rushing creek alongside you, there is composition.

I have stood in few places that challenge yet please my senses so completely as Oak Creek.

Over the next weeks until the mountain winter arrived, one location at a time we began to fill in the spaces on the Forest Service maps I had been inhaling during those long quiet nights behind the front desk of the Weatherford Hotel.

The Plymouth was as advertised. I noticed the oil pressure gauge declining in a regular, repetitive pattern. The leak increased to the extent a quart of oil was required with each tank of gasoline. In another month, it required an additional quart between fill ups. The oil gauge, standard for the time, allowed me to monitor the oil pressure far better than having the oil light. This seemed a minor inconvenience for the services of a vehicle that took us to Foodtown and on day trips through the countryside.

CHAPTER EIGHT

Meanwhile, Back in Stigler

With Billie working at the Telephone Company, communication with Mother and Dad had become almost exclusively by telephone rather than through the mail. The telephone allowed much closer contact with James, Mom and Dad, as well as my grandmothers.

It was during such a conversation we first learned of my folks' distress over James and his perpetually bumpy relationship with Wilma Sunday. James had been dating her at least since the fall of 1957. Between Mom and Dad and the girlfriend, James sounded in a consistent and constant state of trauma and adolescent angst.

He called on Saturday mornings, weekend long distance rates being less expensive, after football Friday nights. I would hear of Hunky Turrentine, Guy Curry, Gam Williams, Don Satterfield, and Gene Basta. Other times, he would be so distressed by interpersonal events I would mostly hear of a variety of parental and peer conflicts that seemed to now fill his life. James seemed persistently perplexed in his attempts to please his emotional triad: Mother, Dad, and Wilma.

It seemed that Hunky and Guy provided sound peer council which he most often chose to ignore.

Still, on the good mornings, I enjoyed the conversations with my brother.

For reasons I did not understand, Mom and Dad disapproved of the relationship between James and Wilma. They so disapproved that during one of what seemed from my distance to be numerous break ups, they purchased him a 1956 Chevy they knew he coveted. A condition of the purchase was he would not renew the relationship with Wilma. As you would expect, this bribery attempt was a complete and utter failure. James was soon picking his date up in his 1956 Chevy.

I was simply too far removed to have any genuine understanding of my parent's concerns.

To talk to Mema Mac was intricate, requiring a cautious sensitivity. She wanted to talk about Granddaddy, but an ill conceived word would bring all of her thoughts and emotions about him spilling out. I could only grasp the edges of the magnitude of her loneliness. I missed him, but I never felt I was without him while Mema was adrift.

Physically, her arthritis was becoming increasingly disabling. There was beginning to be talk of fitting her with braces, devices that sounded like those I had only seen with someone who had recovered from polio. I didn't like that much.

Although she had been emotionally and economically dependent on Granddaddy for most of her life, the thought of losing her independence troubled her. She knew her ability to sustain it was rapidly diminishing. These concerns deepened her sadness.

Mema Lane, my maternal grandmother, continued her dynamic and symbiotic relationship with Aunt Vivian and Uncle Hubert, her eldest daughter and her husband. Mema Lane tended to the household tasks while Aunt and Uncle operated the Stigler 5 & Up.

This arrangement always seemed to work well for all of them.

In the midst of this agreeably gratifying and somewhat harried summer, we got pregnant.

Billie told me in early September, around her birthday. With the unsophisticated confidence of youth, I was first speechless, then amazed, and then ecstatic.

I'm not convinced Billie was pleased with my being so pleased.

CHAPTER NINE

The Deep Woods

During the fall of 1958, I was able to obtain a resident hunting license. After several uneventful early morning hunts near Flagstaff, I was invited on a three day hunt in the country to the northeast of Mormon Lake. Birch Drake, also a Cottage City resident, organized the hunt. Raised in the mountains surrounding Silver City, New Mexico, he was an experienced woodsman and a good camp cook.

Lamar was going on a hunt deep in the Kaibab National Forest on the north rim of the Grand Canyon. Before he left, he gave me some instructions hunting the juniper canyons and pine topped mesas of the area where I was headed.

We all had our deer tags. We pooled our money and bought one bear tag, just in case.

Traveling by pickup truck, first following forest service roads and then no roads at all, noting landmarks as we passed, we made camp shortly before dark in or near a location Birch had camped the previous season. Wood was gathered and cut. A substantial stone circle with a skillet pullout was constructed. The grass was cleared some distance around the site before a fire was built, and what a splendid fire it was.

The nights were clear and cold. The stars appeared to be brighter and closer than any I had ever seen. I was certain it was an optical illusion, but there just seemed to be more stars in the sky than I ever remember.

I slept on the ground in a blanket roll as close to the fire as I dared. The side of my body closest to the fire was the warmer. I think I turned like I was on a spit.

I awakened the next morning well before daylight. Under Birch's instruction, canned biscuits were cooked in deep fat,

Billie and the Boys

bacon fried, and then a dozen eggs with liberal splashes of Tabasco sauce were scrambled.

A solid northern breeze carried the smells from our fire to the south, and we moved north to check an abandoned stock tank. Continuing north, first appearing as mesas, the mouths of several small slot canyons began to appear. With directions selected, paths acknowledged, and landmarks for an afternoon meeting agreed upon, we separated. Within minutes I was completely alone.

I was working about half way up the west side of a somewhat narrow canyon when I picked up a game trail. I followed the trail, spotted fresh signs, and slowed my pace. The canyon was narrowing. Movement across the canyon caught my eye, and I stopped.

One shot of about fifty yards across the canyon killed the deer. Excited, I hustled down to the canyon floor and up the east wall to the dead animal, killed with an incredibly lucky head shot.

I fired the signal shots into the air. By the time I finished field dressing the deer, one of my companions arrived. We cut what we judged to be a strong limb and carried the deer back to camp.

The next day, on top of a mesa, I came upon a deer carcass near a large tree with its bark torn and sporting long deep vertical gashes made by a bear raking his claws. The height and the depth of the tree's scars impressed me. The level of raw power suggested was both mesmerizing and concerning. Confronted with such circumstances, a strange ambivalence rises. I very much wanted to see the animal while having no desire to even be on the same mesa with this bear.

For two days, the only sign I saw of another human being beyond our small group were hoof prints where a man on a shod horse had passed before the last rainfall. I love the idea of these places where no one seems to have been.

Why do I chronicle a deer hunt as part of these stories? The quality of the question merits an explanation.

In 1958, ASC allowed residents of married housing who had been successful during the hunt to suspend the curing carcass for up to a week from the beams of their porch. In our case, the deer hung outside the living room window. You could not enter nor exit our unit without passing it.

Now Billie was so adequately pregnant that my prize kill hanging on our porch only brought her waves of nausea. Oops!

Neighbors offered to pay for the butchering and the sausage in exchange for one half of the venison. I agreed. The deer left. Packages of ground venison cut with sausage and some good venison steaks returned. Billie paled at the thought of the contents of the packages.

Slowly realizing the dilemma, I offered our venison to Connie and Lamar, who now lived off campus. Lamar had killed two deer during his Kaibab hunt, so they declined. Other married students were thrilled to share in our bounty.

Although she was game enough to cook it for me, Billie was never able to eat the venison, and to this day, she claims the thought of it gags her.

CHAPTER TEN

Christmas 1958

During our Thanksgiving Day telephone call, Dad asked if we thought we might come home for Christmas. He said if we could come to Stigler, he would buy the gasoline and have Denver Rogers dealership repair our Plymouth as our Christmas gift. It seemed a most generous gift.

In talking about the amount of oil the Plymouth was now consuming, Dad's solution was simple. He said, "I'll send you a Sinclair credit card, buy a case of oil for your trunk, and drive David home for Christmas."

At first, Billie and I did not believe we had accrued any paid vacation. Still, we felt we had enough money to make the trip and pay our bills. Billie was almost 5 months pregnant. It was time to go visit.

I had no difficulty getting the time off from the Weatherford. Winters were slow and the time between Christmas and New Year's was the slowest time of winter. Also, Mrs. Hall was accustomed to dealing with college students and their two week Christmas break. In checking, Billie found she had several days of vacation accrued and could be scheduled so that she would only miss a few days' work.

Money for both a trip and Christmas gifts was quite another matter. Billie applied her creative touch. From trading stamps to bartering, our imaginative scramble produced nice gifts including a memorable one for my parents.

Our neighbor Alfred Hicks' brother was a talented and well-known Navajo artist. Alfred aspired to similar success. Cash was limited for us both, so Sally presented Billie with a proposal. We would provide the materials and paints for a watercolor. Alfred would select and use the watercolor board in such a way that he could provide a matted watercolor for Billie and me to give to my parents. He could use the reverse halves to create a watercolor that could be sold to another Cottage City couple. The deal was done.

The ultimate result was Alfred and Sally had enough money to buy gifts for their family and we had a fine gift for Mom and Dad.

Alfred's work hung in my parent's home until the house was sold. It how hangs in the home of our youngest son and daughter-in-law.

Alfred became a successful Arizona educator whose art work I understand was always in demand. I doubt any of his works were more appreciated than was his buffalo hunt watercolor during the Christmas season of 1958.

Billie had begun to trade books of S&H Green Stamps that had made the journey west with us to wives from the valley for books of the Gold Bond stamps we acquired in Flagstaff, mostly at Foodtown. Gradually, between bartering and Billie's resourceful use of trading stamps, acceptable Christmas gifts begin to emerge.

Lamar told me about getting a tree permit from the Forest Service. I got the permit and Lamar and I went to a location not far from Lake Mary. I selected what I considered to be the perfect spruce. We both cut Christmas trees. Cutting a Christmas tree was one of the real treats of living in northern Arizona.

When I got the tree back into our unit, I discovered that what appeared to be just the perfect size tree when viewed on the mountain side could occupy half of a living room. This tree did.

But I was so proud of the tree I was reluctant to trim it. Billie understood my pride in this freshly hewed tree. She patiently waited until I came to realize that a Christmas tree with a limb obstructing our front door might be a little too large.

I walked around to Connie and Lamar's unit and borrowed a bow saw to shorten our tree. After a couple of trims, it became a very nice size. Billie had bought a new string of lights to go with the meager decorations we had collected in our two previous Christmases. It was a beautiful Christmas tree.

If the sensory experiences from the sight and fragrance of a freshly cut spruce didn't fill our home with the Christmas spirit, a roughly thirty inch snow fall in the middle of December nudged it right along. I was still marveling at the Flagstaff snowfalls with the large plush flakes that drifted from the sky like the proverbial feather and seemed to settle one on top of the other.

The snow started falling in the early afternoon. I was working at the Weatherford and had to move my car from the street so that the snow plows could begin to work on Aspen Street. I moved it to a space behind the hotel normally reserved for special guests.

As the evening wore on, I found myself repeatedly stepping from behind the desk and walking to the front door and then to the north windows, fascinated by the falling and collecting flakes. Then the snow plows appeared, relocating the snow from the middle of the street nearer to the curb. I gawked as a blower followed by a dump truck came into view. The snow was lifted from the street and deposited into the bed of the dump truck. As one dump truck was filled, another replaced it. This was quite different from snow removal in Stigler.

My shift finished at eleven. I put on my grey cloth coat, quite heavy by Oklahoma standards, and brown jersey gloves. I opened the back door and the view from the top of the steps stopped me cold in my tracks. A glance toward the Plymouth and I retraced my steps, calling Billie that I would be a tad delayed, then secured a broom and shovel from the cleaning closet.

I shoveled a path to the car through the drifted snow and started it to heat and hopefully help to clear the snow from the windows. I swept the car while it warmed. The snow was unexpectedly easy to sweep from car. It was simply much drier that the wet, heavy snows of eastern Oklahoma.

I noted the need for warmer, more water resistant gloves at some future date.

I eased out of the parking lot and made my way down Beaver Street, which was relatively flat toward the college. The drifts in front of our north facing unit were already substantial. Other residents had already parked in the seemingly sheltered area to the east of the building, so I parked as close to the south side of the two story complex to the north of us as I could.

Billie had plugged in the lights on our Christmas tree. Christmas tree lights framing a window and reflecting through the soft fluffy falling mountain snow created as welcoming a winter homecoming sight as you might imagine.

The next morning, I was reminded there are times in life when dumb luck is superior to astute planning. Morning found our car coated by several inches of fresh snow but basically in as good condition as when I parked it the evening before. The strategically parked cars along the east wall were now buried in a door-sealing mixture of snow and slush deposited by the plows blended with below zero temperatures.

For the next two days, the temperatures stubbornly clung at zero or below. Until their vehicles emerged from their frozen tombs, I drove our neighbors to work and to the grocery.

The snowfall must have come on a Saturday because I remember on Sunday evening, my night off, Billie and I dressed David in his almost outgrown snow suit. We walked across campus to Old Main. The campus sidewalks were sufficiently cleared as were the steps of the building. We sat on the steps and watched the cars pass on Route 66, outlined against a backdrop of Christmas lights and flashing neon.

Before I went to work on the Saturday before our departure, I filled up the Plymouth, bought a case of oil along with 3 cans of an oil additive so thick it seemed to barely pour. I dropped a beer can opener into the case of oil. I declared the Plymouth ready to undertake Route 66.

Well before sunrise on the Sunday before Christmas Day on Thursday, we begin our journey.

Now almost 14 months old, David was ready for a road trip. There he sat between Billie and me with both legs poking out of his cloth car seat hooked over the bench seat of the car. As the car straightened out from making a sharp right angle turn on the east side of Holbrook, the sun appeared. If flying feet can be a valid measure, David liked the sunrise. With the sun suddenly directly in my eyes, I'm sure I said something rather inappropriate and pulled the visor down.

I know my sons are convinced the first highway signs I read to them were historical markers. They are wrong. The first signs I read to them were Burma Shave signs. There would always be some familiar landmarks along the path, but the Burma Shave signs were a constant.

The Burma Shave Company arranged small signs in a series providing messages of wisdom, wit, and warning. The warnings were not-so-subtle tips concerning highway safety. All were intended to interest a car's occupants in buying a blue tube of Burma Shave.

On curves ahead
Remember, sonny
That rabbit's foot
Didn't save
The bunny
Burma Shave

Driving to Stigler on Route 66 during the Christmas season of 1958 provided us with what a holiday traveler hoped for in a Christmas journey. The road seemed filled with California plates headed east. The sighting of gifts wrapped in colorful Christmas paper in the back window of a car convinced us that others were making a pilgrimage similar to our own.

Hal Shearon McBride Jr.

The drive through downtown Albuquerque with all its stop lights was more irritating than interesting. My thought was that if we could just clear the main street of Albuquerque, it was open sailing to Amarillo which really wasn't much more than a bump in the road.

What I considered open sailing in 1958 on Route 66 is quite different from today. Even on the open flatlands of New Mexico and the Texas panhandle, travelers seemed to cluster into groups of three or four cars. The highway was two lanes. It seemed you were continually attempting to pass a car, or vice versa. Trucks were uniquely troublesome.

> Is he
> Lonesome
> Or just blind—
> The guy who drives
> So close behind?
> Burma Shave

I don't understand why, but the full extent of the distance we were traveling on these trips always seemed to hit me when we would change time zones in eastern New Mexico. But I always knew we were in Oklahoma when I could buy a Grapette. So, somewhere about Sayre we would stop for gas and Grapette.

We left Route 66, taking a road less traveled that provided a more direct route into Norman. There we would find 9 Highway which took us to Stigler.

Eufaula contained recognizable landmarks. Whitefield brought comfortably familiar sights. We slowed as we entered this crossroads community.

The lights of Maxwell's Store had been turned off for the evening, but the lights of a car in its parking lot were distracting. From a distance, they appeared to belong to a car traveling in the wrong lane. As we approached, the car started honking and flashing the headlights. The driver's door opened. There was James, standing on the door frame and waving his right arm in the air.

I slowed and swung back into the parking lot. James literally ran toward our car. Our welcome home began in the gravel parking lot of Maxwell's Store.

Billie and the Boys

Wilma was in the passenger's seat. Billie and I knew her from our fall in Stigler. She was pleasant but mildly irritated with James. It seems that he had been driving back and forth on Number 9 since late afternoon looking for a green and black Plymouth with Arizona front plates.

He put his arm around my shoulder and asked, "What do you think of her?"

I suppose a little apprehensive from the telephone tales, I responded, "James, Wilma has always seemed pleasant enough."

He laughed and said, "I meant my Chevy."

It was good to see my brother. You can be assured reminders of this exchange provided us with laughter for years to come.

We knew Mother and Dad were waiting. We quickly covered the 6 miles from Whitefield to Stigler.

After almost a year, it was nice to see my parents. Mother and Dad were clearly ecstatic about having their grandchild back in their home.

My grandparents' house was already dark. The fact that my Grandfather was gone took a sudden tangible form that was promptly washed away in my parents' pure joy to have us home for Christmas.

Mother was so proud of the flocked Christmas tree that she had personally selected at the Boy's Club in Fort Smith. The process by which my mother selected a Christmas tree was neither capricious nor hurried.

Once purchased, the tree had been watchfully loaded into the back of the station wagon and unloaded with care. Mother was always took great pride in her Christmas tree.

She was also quick to point out any other Christmas tree in the family that would be required viewing. This year it was Aunt Vivian and Uncle Hubert's stylish aluminum tree adored with candle shaped bubble lights. A disk with panes of green, blue, and red plastic now rotated beneath the tree. The tree appeared to change colors as the disk moved over a light contained in its base.

Mema Lane never really approved of either tree but said so only in the most subtle of ways. We were sitting at the kitchen table at Vivian and Hubert's, and I made some off-hand remark about how nice the trees were.

She responded, "Oscar always cut our trees himself." She was thoughtful, and then added, "Enjoyed stringing the red berries and popcorn. Looked like they belonged on a tree."

She would muse, "Those were real Christmas trees."

You always knew where you stood with Mema Lane.

"Life's too short for folks to be guessin'."

She was direct and unwavering in the expression of her thoughts about most things, but I somehow always felt she was really talking about letting people know you cared about them.

On the other hand, this tiny woman was straight forward and sturdy. Later, when she broke her hip on two separate occasions, she was told by knowing physicians that she would never walk again. Without flinching she responded, "Yes, I will".

And each time she did. Such was her way.

It was our intent to sleep late Tuesday morning, but I awakened early when I heard James start his car to go duck hunting. Ordinarily, I would have simply moved closer to Billie, but this morning I got up. I dressed quietly, went to the kitchen and drank the tad of coffee James couldn't squeeze into his thermos. With arrival of solid daylight and the expiration of the coffee, I left the house.

I thought I would walk to the Stigler Cemetery, but I just didn't move my legs in that direction. I walked to the WPA gym. I tried the doors but they were locked. I read the bronze marker embedded in the stone and tried to remember the men of the Board of Education in 1936. Schuler Gamble was a man I feel I should know but I have no recollection of him. Chet Norman had a first class dry goods store between the First National Bank and the post office. Claud Bell had the pharmacy, and I remember him well, but not as well as A. J. Holland who had rewarded my first feeble attempt at skipping school with a solid paddling with a board I try not to recall. And yes, Dad whipped me again that night.

C. W. Berner remains a mystery to me.

I sat on the stoop of the gym with my own thoughts. Finally, I acknowledged to myself that I was not going to the cemetery that morning.

Billie and the Boys

I walked back home. Billie and Mother were now busy in the kitchen. Dad was emerging from the hallway dressed in a starched shirt and crisply creased khaki pants, freshly showered and ready for a day at the shop. My dad really loved his shop. He enjoyed visiting with the people who would come and go. He liked to show others his knowledge of his voltmeter and tube checker. It was the tedious work he bemoaned.

Then, James came in the back door grumbling about a fruitless morning of pond hopping. Dad told him that he was hunting the wrong ponds and told where he should have gone. James bristled. I sipped my coffee and thought things hadn't changed much.

As she is wont to do, Billie smiled and ask me what I thought, trying to bait me into that futile discussion.

I said, "I think I'd like to go duck hunting with James before we leave."

There was an odd silence. It was not the idea that I wanted to go hunting my brother, but the concept that we were going to leave was introduced when we had just barely arrived.

Mother said, "I going to come stay with you when the new baby gets here." No discussion, just a statement of fact.

I did go duck hunting with my brother before we left. Now James and I had hunted together often. I still enjoy telling stories of him crawling for yards across open fields of frost-covered grass to slip up over the dam of some small prairie pond just in the event that a mallard or two might be lurking just out of sight. Given due deliberation, any thinking person might have concluded ducks were my brother's mortal enemies, a genuine threat to civilization as we knew it.

Our December duck hunt remains such a poignant memory that it is the only story I choose to retell in this writing.

I took our car to the shop at Denver Rogers Chrysler Plymouth dealership. Then, I took my Freeman cordovan wing-tips, my one good pair of shoes, to Everett Bidwell and left them for new heels and half-soles.

Billie and I took David next door to visit Mema Mac. I tried to visit with her but the absence of my grandfather was simply overwhelming for both of us. The words stumbled for both of us.

She held my hand and said, "You are so much like him."

I responded far too quickly, "Yes and no." I slowed myself and said what she wanted to hear, "More yes than no."

She patted my hand. Then, she became completely engaged in Billie's descriptions of our life in Flagstaff in the precise detail that only one woman can convey to another woman.

Billie is still the most skilled observer of her environment I know.

Lou came over that afternoon. She drove Billie and David to Sallisaw. I would come over the next afternoon, Christmas Eve.

Christmas was celebrated on Christmas Eve night in Lou and Charles' home. Mattox Christmases were always fun and formal. All of Billie's sisters and their husbands were there. This was only my second one, and I was still feeling my way into the flow of the evening, but Billie loved these Christmas gatherings with her sisters.

While there might be some his equal, I don't believe anyone enjoyed Christmas mornings more than my father. He couldn't stay in the bed much past five AM despite my mother's best efforts to control him. Christmas mornings found my father in his glory.

He would go to the kitchen. There he would put on the coffee and place some type of sweet rolls in the oven. If you ignored the aroma of Folgers coffee and the loud clanking of pots and pans in kitchen, then he would actually come to the bedroom.

He would whistle, creating an ear-piercing sound that had once been used to summon James and me home from blocks away. The sound virtually echoed through the house and the head.

Now convinced he had some type of audience, he'd yell, "Santa's been here!"

This was a combination guaranteed to awaken any child. It extracted groans, along with substantial derogatory commentary from every other adult in the house except my mother.

The smell emanating from the two fresh perked pots of Folgers continued to creep through the hallway and met you as you emerged from the bedroom.

It seemed almost instantaneous, but my mother would have retrieved the orange juice pitcher from the refrigerator and began stirring it. At Daddy's encouragement, she clanged the large spoon into the side of the pitcher, creating a bell effect. She would be setting out small glasses, several of which had contained chipped beef in a previous life, by the pitcher. She would hand a glass of orange juice to each member of the family as they made their way into the kitchen. It was at such times I had no question as to how genuinely happy my mother was.

This morning, as on all Christmas mornings, I can remember at 607 NW "A" Street, Dad had closed the doors adjoining the kitchen and the living room. The kitchen was abuzz with excited children while frazzled adults sipped on hot Folgers and hoped for the best.

The Christmas morning of 1958 was no exception. My father was thrilled to once again have a child in the room.

From the bedroom window, I could see Mema Mac's bedroom light was already on next door. Daddy had called her. Her crippling arthritis now made the simplest of movements a struggle for her and would soon put her in braces. The doors to the living room, to the Christmas tree, would not be opened until she was seated, her coffee and orange juice on a table by her side. While she would live to see three more Christmas Days, I believe she would have considered this to be her last.

David, at 14 months, had the concept that what was on the other side of those doors was exciting. He was right.

He got a red Radio Flyer wagon, a football, and a small train that traveled in circles. The gift that ultimately enthralled him was a yellow turtle whose green head bobbed in and out as it was rolled across the floor. He pushed the turtle all over Mom and Dad's house. The turtle completely captivated him.

Later, at home in Cottage City, he pushed that turtle all over the unit. The turtle almost replaced a round plastic ball he had received for his birthday and his beloved enamel dishpan.

Mother prized the Buffalo Hunt watercolor that Alfred had painted. Billie and I were very proud of the gift. Over the years, it grew on Daddy. Still, in his mind, it never acquired the esthetic beauty of his two mounted bass.

The smells of sausage, bacon, and ham frying would now overwhelm the remaining scent of perking coffee. Soon, the breakfast table would be surrounded by clattering family. The meats along with eggs, waffles, and sausage gravy would be devoured. The chatter of family talking all at the same time and over each over consumed the room.

Hal Shearon McBride Jr.

Above all other gatherings, my Daddy and Mother loved Christmas morning. They shared their excitement with us all.

On Christmas Eve, James and I had decided we would go duck hunting the morning after Christmas. I purchased a license and a duck stamp before leaving for Sallisaw.

We left the house well before daybreak, stopping at Don's Café to fill two thermos bottles with coffee and set out for the Kinta prairie. Pond hopping on the prairie was unproductive, so we made our way back toward Martin Box School, a one room school to the northwest of Stigler. As we turned back east, the sun in our eyes, James pulled over, indicating there was a small pond just beyond view from the road. We made our way down a rather steep bar ditch and through a rusting barbed wire fence toward a heavily tree lined pond.

For no reason other than its personal significant to me, I will repeat the story as I recorded it in To Bear Witness. The passage began as my Grandfather was in the middle bedroom of his home dying with cancer of the prostate. David was about a month old.

It seems as soon as she could, Billie, along with David, resumed her daily visits with Granddaddy. Shortly after David's arrival, he overheard Billie in the hallway saying to David, "Let's go talk to your Great-Granddaddy, your Granddaddy's crazy."

He repeated that story to all that would listen. I am certain Dad Bankhead, who was an almost daily visitor, heard it more times than he would care to recall.

And he loved to tell the story of one of his last duck hunts with James. At the time, shotgun shells purchased by the case came in a very sturdy wooden box. He had a padded seat created for one end of a Remington shell case, an accommodation to the discomfort of the advancing prostate cancer. This would allow him to sit in a blind on a pond. On this hunt, James flushed three ducks. They each got one on the rise and Granddaddy shot the third out from under James.

James angrily turned to him and blurted, "Granddaddy, you old fart, you shot my duck!" Granddaddy loved it.

The December after Granddaddy's death, Billie and I had returned to Stigler from Flagstaff for the Christmas holiday. James and I went duck hunting. We jumped five mallards on a pond, three

Billie and the Boys

rose my way and two broke to James' side. We both knocked down two; I got the third as it was flying over the dam. Then I realized that James' gun was in front of me. He was so good that he could have shot that third mallard, but he let me have the shot.

I looked at him and said, "You know the old fart would have shot that duck out from under me?"

We both laughed until our sides literally hurt as we collected the three ducks that had hit on land, then sat on the bank and drank coffee from a thermos as the breeze carried the two ducks that had landed on the pond drifted nearer to us. We talked of Granddaddy.

I like to think we both knew there was something unique about that morning, about that shoot. We went to the house and Billie took pictures of us holding the ducks.

That was the last time my brother and I were to hunt together. I still find pleasure in those pictures.

After lunch and planning to leave early the next morning, I knew I had delayed a visit to the cemetery as long as I could. Billie offered to go with me. It was one of the rare times I declined a walk with my wife.

I suspect at a most measured pace, I proceeded to the cemetery. Where now six of my family lie buried beneath an orderly and unobtrusive row of modest grey marble headstones, then there were only two, my Great-Grandmother Missouri Emily McBride and my Grandfather.

While one season of spring rains and a summer's growth of grass had smoothed the plot to a degree, the ground still appeared disturbed. I picked a rather large clump of the clay-like soil and crumbled it in my hand, allowing the grains to fall onto the grave. I repeated this with several of the larger clumps as I slowly walked around the grave, somewhat transfixed by the inscription of his name on the headstone.

I was as silent as my surroundings. It felt real yet not. I felt sad yet I wasn't.

His stone matched his mother's well enough. He had carefully selected her stone and during our visits to her gravesite he was adamant that his stone and that of Mema Mac should match Missouri Emily's stone. My Dad had done well.

For that matter, with one exception over the years and with the assistance of first Lloyd Munn and then Doug Martin, good men both, the matching of the stones has been acceptable.

I ground the last large clod of dirt with my hand. When the last of it had fallen on the grave, I stood just a moment. Then, I walked back to Mother and Dad's home.

Granddaddy left only one other post-life directive. "If you can't put live flowers on my grave, don't put any at all." Each Memorial Day weekend, Billie and I place live flowers by each headstone.

I still linger at their graves.

After lunch, I rode back to town with Dad. We visited in the shop a bit and then I went across the street to see Aunt Vivian and Uncle Hubert. I had seen them before Christmas but with the demise of the school book trade as free books became available to students in the public schools, the Christmas season was now essential to the survival of the Stigler 5 & Up. I had assembled a couple of tricycles and swept out the store one evening, but the season had limited the quality of our visits.

This day after Christmas the store was empty. There was some reorganization of merchandise taking place, but it was calm. Aunt Vivian was filling the samplers of some fragrances, Blue Waltz and Apple Blossom, I suspect. Aunt was conscientious about having the samplers full for the young girls. She found satisfaction in watching their smiles and giggles as they tested the samplers.

My uncle, as always in his white shirt and tie, was at the desk behind the candy counter working on what appeared to be a bank deposit. Billie and I took Emily Ann and visited him in a nursing home a few weeks before his death in 1990. He was wearing a white shirt and tie.

Aunt Vivian and I took a Coke and went behind the curtain into the stock room. Auntie and I sat on boxes and talked. It was the first time she smoked a cigarette in front of me. We both had a good laugh about the times I would disrupt her and her friends during their recreational smoke. But mostly, I recall the talk as being more serious and about the success of the Christmas season.

I left the store and walked toward Hays and Buchanan which, like the cemetery, I had avoided. I window shopped the store, came back to the entrance to the men's side and hesitated. I was lost, staring into the tiles leading to the front door. I started to step away when Eulis LaFave opened the door and with the warmest of handshakes, invited me inside. I don't know if he had seen me standing outside, but I will forever be grateful to him inviting me inside.

We sat in the shoe department. He told me of their Christmas season in great depth. The only specific I recall from the conversation was his concern about the future of S&H Green Stamps. I told him that trading stamps were important to us in grocery shopping and that we had used them to secure some Christmas gifts this year.

Discount stores were barely lurking on the horizon.

He spoke of things he had learned from my Grandfather. When we were done, we again shook hands and wished each other good luck. I really wanted to hug the man and thank him, but I didn't. I don't know that Eulis ever understood the great kindness of his act.

CHAPTER ELEVEN

The Stormy Road Home

The mechanic at Rogers Motor was not quite finished with our car but promised it by noon on Saturday, so we resigned ourselves to a later departure and an arrival in Flagstaff on Monday in time for me to go to work at 3 PM.

We finally left about mid-afternoon, making our way west on highway 9 until we again joined Route 66 in Sayre. Enjoying a new found sense of confidence in the Plymouth, I was pressing for time while enjoying the oil pressure gage remaining in the same location for miles on end.

A guy
Who drives
A car wide open
Is not thinkin'
He's just hopin'
Burma Shave

Supper was a hamburger at what over the years would become our favorite Route 66 Dairy Queen in Shamrock, Texas.

We made Amarillo near midnight and found a small motel on the west side of town. Billie and I were physically and emotionally tired, and David was just plain tired.

I walked David back to sleep and Billie put him down. We ate the sandwiches Billie and Mother had prepared before we left Stigler. We talked and laughed about our visit. Then, we fell into a deep sleep.

We slept soundly, but awakened briskly with a wake-up call from the front desk. David, usually a reliable early morning alarm, had slept. A glance out the window revealed a dusting of snow covering the grassy surfaces while leaving the pavement only damp. A step outside the room and it was evident it had gotten noticeably colder. The snow seemed to be blowing from the east, so I told Billie I thought we might drive out of it.

It is safe to assume that weather forecasting in 1958 was not what it is today. Weather reports told us what the weather had been, not what it was going to be.

By the time we reached the feedlots of Wildorado, the snow was increasing. It remained steady through Tucumcari and Santa Rosa but 66 remained reasonably clear. We pulled over in Santa Rosa and filled up with gasoline. The owner said he believed the road on into Albuquerque was about like what we had traveled over.

Between Santa Rosa and Clines Corners the blizzard hit. I had driven us into the storm, not out of it.

The snow was blowing and visibility was extremely limited. The air was so cold that moisture forming on the inside of windows was freezing, requiring Billie to scrape it away. The traffic was thinning, leaving the impression you were the only car in the storm. We were relieved to see the lights of Clines Corners through the snow.

Clines Corners, New Mexico was really a large truck stop in the middle of the high desert, a truck stop whose population had swelled dramatically in the storm. On this day, it was a truck stop that had sold out of gasoline. The inside of the restaurant was packed with an assortment of people.

There was heat, but the food supply had dwindled, partly consumed by people waiting out the storm and partly because the storm had forced the cancellation of scheduled deliveries. Their remaining menu consisted of cheese sandwiches. We bought four. We also bought the last three half-pints of milk for David's bottle. And looking around us, we felt fortunate.

Billie and I had pretty well decided that we would simply have to remain at Clines Corner until the storm passed. Then, a New Mexico highway patrolman said that about 20 miles to the west, you would drive out of the storm. He was driving that direction and all of us with gasoline and chains who wanted to follow him were welcome. He further assured us that he would not leave anyone stranded.

The patrolman said since we only had a strap chain for our drive wheel we should take the position behind him. As I recall, there were five cars behind us.

For the next hour, I drove behind a New Mexico Hiway Patrol cruiser. Although it tried valiantly, the Plymouth heater was no match for the cold of the blizzard, so Billie continually wiped the moisture from in front of me so that it would not freeze. The wipers were able to sustain only a small opening on the windshield. Once I had to open my window and reach out to free the wipers, but no way was I going to lose sight of that highway patrol car. I have often said since had the patrolman driven out across the desert of New Mexico, I'd have been in his tail pipe.

Then, somewhere between Clines Corner and Albuquerque, as if God had drawn a line, the snow turned to rain and then the pavement was dry. The highway patrolman pulled to the side of the road, waved us over, quickly unhooked our strap chain and put it back in our trunk. He seemed to be counting the cars, being certain he still had the same number of vehicles behind him as when his caravan had left Clines Corner.

I don't know that "terrified" would describe our feelings during that drive, but we were fearful. I do know that I could not have made the drive alone. It was Billie keeping the inside of the window shield clear that was the critical difference. She has never questioned my decision to drive behind the patrol car.

When we stopped in Albuquerque for gasoline, Billie felt she should call Lou and let her know we were alright.

Lou said, "What snow storm?"

I called Mom and Dad. No one in Stigler knew there was a severe blizzard over New Mexico.

Yes, both calls were collect.

Billie and I had another discussion about spending the night in Albuquerque, but we decided we would be spending money that would needed when we got home.

We had little more than pulled out of the gasoline station and our left rear tire went flat. One of the two new recaps we had been given for Christmas failed. I looked at Billie. Billie looked

Billie and the Boys

at me. I'm not certain of my expression, but she giggled, a rare girlish giggle from my wife. I just shook my head.

I changed the tire, started the car and told Billie I sure hoped we didn't have another flat because I didn't have another tire.

> Better try
> Less speed per mile
> That car
> May have to
> Last a while
> Burma Shave

When we hit the city limits of Holbrook, Billie pronounced us to be close enough to Flagstaff to call someone to come and retrieve us. I do not know how or why we have always been able to make each other laugh, but we have.

Billie and David were both sound asleep when I shut off the motor in front of 85 Cottage City. I nudged Billie and said, "We're home, Sweet."

CHAPTER TWELVE

Home Again

We settled back into our routines of work and school. As much as possible, Billie was working early morning shifts or split shifts. I went to classes in the morning and worked at The Weatherford from 3 pm to 11 pm. We wanted one of us to be with David as much as possible while our neighbor, Sally Hicks, covered the odd times.

During the spring semester of 1959, I took a history class, The World Since 1919. It was my first exposure to a serious historian, Garland Downum. He ignited an avid but lately dormant interest in history that had first been sparked by John Harmon at Stigler High School. I have never again allowed that interest to wane.

The contractor for the construction of the diversion tunnels for the Glen Canyon Dam was Merritt, Chapman and Scott. Their foremen, supervisors, and the project manager had become weekend regulars at the Weatherford. This provided a steady and unexpected revenue stream for the hotel during the typically bleak winter months.

They would arrive between 9 and 10 on Friday evening. Having spent the week living and eating in a tent city at the construction site of the dam, they were first interested in showering away the dust.

Most of these men seemed to have their homes and their roots in western Pennsylvania. While I suppose I expected a rowdy lot, they were not. Most were simply lonely, tired men far away from their families, unaccustomed to the acute isolation and unforgiving climate of the Colorado plateau. They just wanted to see a movie, enjoy a late evening meal, and sleep in beds not filled with the gritty, grainy, abrasive sand-dust that covered their site high above the Colorado River.

Mostly, they just missed being home.

One winter evening, David was exercising his prize turtle, pushing it across the floor at a nice pace, under the bucket chair and generally all round the room. Billie was working a shift that allowed her to be home by early evening. I had just finished running the small vacuum across the rug and behind the television.

As I put the vacuum away, I heard a crashing noise and a scream from David that seemed to come at the same time. I found a very frightened David crying and sitting amidst the shattered remains of Billie's prized television lamp. A few of the marbles had rolled around the floor, but most remained encased in the white glass. I lifted David from the devastation, making certain he was just frightened and not injured. I walked him, patting his back and calming him. Then, I put him in his crib.

I viewed the catastrophe. I was heartsick.

After vacuuming, I had not adequately replaced the lamp cord under the television. A cord now draped about the neck of David's turtle. For whatever reason you remember such things, and I collected the loose marbles in a Melmac coffee cup and then began to sort out the larger fragments of the lamp, having a fantasy of restoration in my mind. Then, I realized the pieces were far too small and started retrieving the embedded marbles.

Then I just got a horrible sinking feeling in the pit of my stomach. No matter what I did I wasn't going to be able to make this right. The spam with a sliced pineapple on top I had baking in the oven for dinner was going to provide no salve for this wound.

Do you know how horrible it feels to be responsible for breaking the piece of furniture your wife treasures most? I do, and I still recall it well.

Although Billie made every effort, her face could not hide her sense of loss when she saw the shattered remains of the lamp. She comforted David and tried to reassure me. I guaranteed her we would find another lamp but we couldn't, or I should say haven't.

I still search for a replacement for that lamp.

We were preparing for the arrival of the baby. We used the cash we had been given as Christmas gifts to purchase a very nice crib. We systematically begin adding additional bottles and new diapers to our existing inventory. We bought something new each time either of us got paid.

Billie's insurance with Mountain States provided some very restricted maternity benefits, so since the fall we had been paying five dollars each payday to both the Flagstaff Memorial Hospital and to Dr. John Kahle. We paid Dr. Kahle five dollars over the next several years. I believe he had the majority of the residents of Cottage City on some payment plan or another.

Shortly after our return to Flagstaff, we started to get telephone calls from Mother and Dad, distraught about James. I never understood what they expected me to do. By the end, I believe they preferred to talk to Billie rather than to me.

James and Wilma decided to get married before their graduation from High School in the spring of 1959. I received a very matter of fact telephone call from James. He said that while he suspected I would not be able to come back for the wedding, he wanted to ask me to be his Best Man anyway. I declined and thanked him for asking.

James told me of their plans. James did not ask my opinion, and I volunteered none. I expressed no opinions because I had none. I did wish he might have been marrying under less conflicted circumstances. I only desired the best for my brother, but I did not know what the best was.

Despite Mother's tears and Dad's bitter disappointment, in the spring of 1959, James Lane McBride and Wilma Lee Sunday were married by Wilma's father in his church, the Freewill Baptist Church of Stigler.

They moved in with Mema Mac and completed their high school educations.

The descriptions of the wedding I received from my parents were at best sketchy, those I did get were frankly rather morose. Worse, their voiced concerns did not cease; they simply shifted focus to what was or was not transpiring in Mema Mac's home.

I was glad Billie and I were a thousand miles away.

During our years in Flagstaff, we would make two other trips back to Oklahoma.

One trip would involve Billie's mother, whom I had never met and nothing in the accounts I heard suggested that I should have even the slightest desire to meet the woman. While Charles was non-committal, Jay was adamant that the woman should be allowed back in Billie's life. Initially, my attitude was Billie's attitude; her mother was a non-entity in her life. It is my opinion that the quality of our lives would not have been diminished had she remained in that role.

It seems I must acknowledge I had a head start on not liking this woman.

Billie's mother, Mary Dale Martin Merriott, was the woman who left her nine year-old daughter standing at the railroad station in Vian, Oklahoma. She told Billie that it didn't matter if she went or not, Mary Dale was taking her small son, Mike Merriott, and going to California to be with the father of her son.

Had Jay Reynolds, home for the weekend, not rushed from Sallisaw to Vian, Billie would have been left standing alone watching the train pull away. While Billie's sisters all know the story only too well, Annice's husband, Jay, was the only person who ever really discussed it with me. It was speaking of the drive from Vian to Sallisaw, taking Billie to Lou and Charles's home that seemed to always leave Jay reaching for words. He'd just shake his head no and move on.

Regardless, Lou and Charles opened their home to Billie. On occasion, Billie talked about how one of the first things Charles did was send her on a treasure hunt to find the new bicycle he had purchased for her. The bicycle gave her a feeling of independence.

More importantly, the gift represented acceptance; a tangible proof that somebody noticed she was there and cared. And the bicycle was new.

Bicycles and their symbolism remain so significant to Billie that on a Christmas sixty plus years later, we found ourselves at a Walmart Supercenter buying bicycles for two children whose names had not been chosen from the Angel Tree at the school where our daughter-in-law, Cheryl, teaches. Their cards had gone unselected because their special Christmas wish had been for a more expensive gift: a bicycle. We were told it was quite acceptable to purchase more practical gifts as these children really only expected clothes. Well, it wasn't okay.

I cannot adequately express the delight we got from selecting just the right bicycles, one for a boy and one for a girl. Once chosen, Billie guarded them closely to prevent their selection by another shopper. Woe be to any shopper who attempted to buy one of those bicycles from under her.

So, on a Sunday afternoon, with the school empty, we parked two brand new bicycles beside the Christmas tree at the University School.

It felt a lot like Christmas.

I did ultimately meet Billie's mother, Mary, and her husband, Cecil Merriott, during our time in Flagstaff. I found the encounter disagreeable and I'll leave it there.

I did not see Mary again for over 30 years. I never saw Cecil again.

On the other side of the coin, I will be eternally grateful to Charles Mattox and Jay Reynolds for their loving efforts to aid their wives' baby sister. I realize in the greater karma of life had her mother not abandoned her, I would have never met Billie, and my life would have been infinitely and incalculably the poorer for it.

Perhaps having already said more than I should, I do consider these to be stories Billie alone has the right to tell and I leave it at that.

CHAPTER THIRTEEN

April 1959

After a snowy January and February, March was cold and rainy. Billie had the first of two false labors that were so adequately intense they sent us scurrying to Flagstaff Memorial Hospital. The second of these false labors came in early April and was sufficiently convincing that it resulted in an attempt to induce labor. With the effort appearing to be headed for success, I called Stigler.

By the time we realized this protracted effort was going to fail, Mother had already boarded the train in Muskogee and was headed west. She arrived to find she was to have week of quality time with her eldest grandchild before the new baby arrived.

The delight her eldest grandchild provided was muted by her tearful and troubled accounts of what she referred to as "James' circumstances." The thought of her youngest son's marriage dismayed her.

I confess I was concerned. The events of the pregnancy were beginning to wear on Billie and my Mother's sadness was starting to bear a resemblance of some unfathomable woe. I did believe that she was borrowing trouble where none yet existed.

Billie, who provided my wisest council on such matters, was not at the top of her game. We were in Arizona far away from the actual circumstances. Knowing my parents sheltered James to his determent, I muddled along.

The only inroad I can remember making with my mother involved reminding her that when she and Daddy married, Daddy was the first of the McBride children to marry. I speculated that Granddaddy and Mema Mac might have had a reservation or two about their marriage. She would promptly dismiss any such notions as foolishness, observing those were different times. And they certainly were.

While I never fully understood the correlation, she would say it was really just my dad's elder brother, Howett McBride, who insistently teased her.

We laughed at her retelling of the story of the Thanksgiving Day of 1936, her first in my father's family. Mother had been assigned the responsibility of making the gravy. The gravy turned out a little thick, or a whole lot thick, depending on the personal adaptation of the teller.

With the family properly seated around a formal dining room table where the best of manners were expected, Uncle Howett pondered the gravy bowl in front of him, looked at my dad and asked, "Shearon, would you pass the gravy knife?"

Mother cried. Daddy unleashed a furious verbal outburst.

Uncle Howett led the chorus of laughter. Granddaddy gave his eldest son's knuckles a firm rap with a spoon while reprimanding him by pointing out all the work the women had done in preparing the meal.

Now, mother would smile at the story and concede the gravy was a little thick. Uncle Howett's version was, "My fork stood up in that gravy."

In April of 1959, this tad of family prospective helped little. It was taking care of her eldest grandson while relieving Billie of some of the household chores that gave her periods of good humor.

Billie and the Boys

Billie and I went to the hospital for the third attempt. It was cold and misty with the remnants of an April snowfall still visible under the trees and around the north facing entrance to the hospital.

During the first couple of hours, she seemed to be well on her way to delivery. Then, the contractions begin to slow and Dr. Kahle decided to make another attempt to induce the continuation of labor. So the necessary IVs were put into place, and a prickly nurse advised me there was nothing more useless at the birth of a child than the father. Then she helped Billie into the bathroom

It is at this point that Clint Walker, the star of the then popular television series <u>Cheyenne,</u> merits a mention. Walker was staying in Flagstaff at the Ramada during the filming of his movie, <u>Yellowstone Kelly</u>. It seems that while leaving the motel for a ride on his motorcycle, he had struck and injured a boy who stepped from the curb in front of him.

He had decided though he was not at fault in the accident, a visit to the boy at the hospital would be appropriate. It seems Billie's nurse was an ardent fan. A co-worker hurriedly brought her the news that he was in the building. Being eager to take advantage of the opportunity to meet the star of the program, she handed Billie the IV bag and left her in the bathroom, hustling past my seated irrelevant rear and scurried down the hallway in hopes of catching a glimpse of her hero.

Billie was in the bathroom yelling for the nurse to come back. She needed help. I hurried into the hallway, but all the staff was clustered at the far end. I went back into the room as Billie was exiting the bathroom, pushing the IV stand with her gown untied and dangling off of one shoulder, draped in disarray. She was extremely irritated at all of us for leaving her. She was really pissed!

Only a sudden and unexpected intensification of her labor saved me from the full passion of her wrath. Then, I really got verbally assertive about finding her help as I assisted her back into the bed. Near panic would be an appropriate descriptor.

To those of us who know him so well, it comes as no surprise that James Michael McBride had been resistive to arriving on time. April 17, 1959 presented no exception.

Now fashionably late, Mike arrived in a hurry.

Out of his office for lunch, Dr. Kahle hurriedly covered the distance to the hospital, arriving just in time for the delivery.

He came back to the room where I was waiting and told me the baby was a boy. Then, he prepared me for Billie. She was fatigued not just by the delivery, but also by the sleepless weeks of uncertainty that had preceded Mike's birth. Having been convinced this baby was a girl, she was not taking the news he was a boy well.

She was sobbing when she was returned to the room. Her black hair was wet, curly and falling down her forehead. I straighten her gown and pulled the covers up. She turned toward the wall.

A well-intended nurse, believing that a baby would calm any distraught mother, brought the fresh scrubbed and blanket wrapped Mike, smelling of soap and lotion, into the room. It didn't help.

She started to leave, and I asked if I could hold him. She paused, seemingly unsure. When I told her we had a little one at home, she relented. I sat in a rocking chair situated so that it provided a view of a pine grove bordering the hospital on the west. It had begun to rain.

I have had some outstanding experiences in my life but none ever exceeded my next hour. I cradled Mike's head in my hands and just looked at him. I don't know how long I actually gazed at his still red face and his closed eyes, watching the corner of his lips move ever so slightly. I can tell you it is impossible to describe the emotions that fill you when you first hold your child. It was so unique, an event unto itself.

As much as St. Edwards had shielded David from me as if I were diseased, Flagstaff Memorial Hospital left me alone with my newborn son. We rocked, Mike nestled into my shoulder and I talked to him. I told him how much I loved him, how happy I was to see him, and how overjoyed I was to be holding him. For whatever reason you do such things, I softly voiced my dad's favorite lullaby to him, "Frankie and Johnnie." An odd song for a lullaby, but it has been sung to every child in our family since my father sang it to my brother and me.

Billie and the Boys

It would be difficult to hold anyone any closer than I held Mike in that rocking chair, looking out the window at the pine trees in a spring rain.

Billie must have watched us for a while. When the nurse came to retrieve Mike, Billie reached out and asked for him. She held him close and began to tear. Anyone who tells you there is no difference in the tears of happiness and the tears of distress was not in that hospital room.

I asked the nurse to leave Mike a bit longer. She nodded. Billie snuggled him into her shoulder and rubbed his back in a circular motion.

The nurse took him back to the nursery. We had chosen the name before his arrival but hadn't settled on what we would call him. I ask Billie if she thought he was a James or Michael.

"A Michael. Mike."

So it has been.

Exhausted, Billie dozed off. I kissed her cheek, and it tasted salty. I touched her still damp hair.

I went to the nursery and just looked at Mike through the window for the longest of times. He was healthy and perfect. I couldn't wait to get him home.

I can't remember the name we had chosen had he been a girl, but I remember the day as clearly as if it was yesterday.

I stepped out of the hospital. The pine laden mountain air felt and smelled exactly as it should have on such a grand and glorious occasion.

I missed a class the next morning to go back to the hospital and rock him.

James Michael McBride came home to 85 Cottage City.

His nursery was our bedroom. Our bed was in the center of the room flanked by a crib on each side. Our sons are 18 months apart. Our small bedroom was compact, providing an inevitable sense of togetherness. The personal space was limited, but I really liked the unique intimate warmth it afforded. We were up close and personal.

My mother's gloom lifted with the arrival. Dad couldn't drive the route quickly enough to see his new grandson and to retrieve his wife.

In the spring of 1959, our life was caring for our infant son, playing with David, work, and school.

Billie and I formed a routine that became a well-established ritual: the day shift with the boys was hers, and the night time awakenings were all mine. I admit that handling the night duties was not a great inconvenience for me. I awaken easily and just as promptly return to sleep. Beyond the practical, I considered the late night feedings and diaper changes followed by the rocking of a son to be among the best of times.

During the late evenings, we would sit on our couch and watch television. 77 Sunset Strip, Gunsmoke, and Have Gun Will Travel were regular viewing, but it was the comedies that we so enjoyed watching together, Red Skelton and Danny Thomas. There are few balms in life that surpass the restorative powers of shared laughter.

CHAPTER FOURTEEN

Cottonseed Hulls

As golfers are prone to do, especially those of us who have reached a point that we hit a garden hoe and a 7 iron about the same distance and with approximately the same accuracy, there is the inevitable dialogue about courses we would like to play. The expected Augusta National Golf Club, the Old Course at St. Andrew's, Pebble Beach, or some other desired course always makes its appearance. I am never completely honest in these fanciful musings.

The golf course I most want to play no longer exists except in my mind. I know it well, and I revisit it often. I have been known to carefully sketch the course layout on a note pad while attending a seminar in which I was especially disinterested.

I want to play Flagstaff Country Club.

The course really has nothing to recommend it beyond my wonderful memories of my introduction to the game. Although I can't seem to recall exactly when I first went to Flagstaff Country Club, I know I was void of expectations. Not only had I never played golf, I had never knowingly seen a golf course.

I know it was in the spring of 1959. Spring comes late at 6900 feet. I know the course had not yet opened for the summer season because we could play for free. There were no flags on the putting surfaces, and there were still patches of snow in the pine groves that lined the fairways. Let me say again, we could play for free.

Flagstaff Country Club was located just off highway 180, the back road to the Grand Canyon, a stretch of two-lane road providing the knowing traveler with views of Kendrick Peak and the San Francisco Peaks. Having just lost a large number of its membership to the newly constructed Coconino Country Club with its seductive grass greens and lush watered fairways, Flagstaff Country Club had become affordable.

Flagstaff Country Club, now made up of a group of die hard older members and newcomers who could not have otherwise afforded the game, provided an environment in which a beginner could learn the game and fully enjoy the experience. It created a rich blend of Flagstaff retirees who had grown up on the course and those of us brought to Flagstaff by the college.

The clubhouse was a large log structure. If it was not built in part of pines harvested from the property, then it should have been. The large east facing screened porch provided a view of 8 fairway and 9 green. I have no idea why it was screened because Flagstaff had few bugs. The bar, grill, and pro shop were just inside the porch. To the north of the bar, grill, and pro shop was the dining room. While its furnishings were quite dated, those who knew about such things raved about the wood of the sizable dance floor.

It was on this course I discovered the addictive properties of golf, a game than entices, promises, and humbles, all on a single swing of the club; a game that promptly revives hope after the most humbling of results.

The obsessive properties of golf continue to beguile me despite the limitations of a very arthritic upper spine and a substantial surgery on L1 through L4 that make an effective return to the game doubtful. Even knowing that it is improbable that I will ever be able to swing as I once did, just the fantasy of a round on LaFortune or Mohawk brings a motivation to the necessary rehabilitative activities in my life. Golf retains its grip on my imagination.

I suppose Flagstaff Country Club required imagination in and of itself. The tee boxes were all elevated. In fact, they were constructed of logs and filled with dirt. There was no grass to be found on any tee box on the course. However, the dirt was firm but not packed solid. A tee was easily placed into the soil, unlike some grass covered tee boxes that I have since played on an Oklahoma August day that virtually required a tack hammer to drive a tee into them.

Billie and the Boys

No grass would found on the "greens" of Flagstaff Country Club, either. The putting surfaces were made of oiled, pressed cottonseed hulls that were rolled a couple of times each day. While they were spongy, they still received a reasonably struck shot well enough. They putted slow, but were passably true.

Not surprisingly, the grass in the fairways was spotty, but again acceptable for play. Local rules always allowed for the ball to be moved to the closest grass, no closer to the hole. The fairways would be reseeded each spring and fall with Kentucky bluegrass, but it was the hardy native grass that is found the mountain meadows of northern Arizona that dominated the fairways. The fairways were blend of islands of grass and small rocks, some cinder-like in nature.

Balls were generally scuffed and nicked after a few holes, but it was okay. We were playing golf.

On occasion I hear people complain about the relative quality of a golf course, expressing displeasure that the grass on the greens is inconsistent, or it has bare places, or that the fairways are spotty. I rarely say anything to my companions, but I always, always think, "Guys, we're getting to play golf." While I will certainly concede some courses are more pleasant to play than others, there are no bad golf courses. It is all about playing the game on the course that is available to you.

Lamar Haines, the Wilson Sporting Goods representative for the region and who was involved with Tissaw's Sporting Goods, was likely tiring of loaning me his clubs. A Tissaw's customer had ordered a set of Wilson's Sam Snead Blue Ridge. This was the bottom of the Wilson golf club line. The customer promptly decided that they didn't meet his golfing standards. He returned them and bought a set of Wilson Staffs and left Tissaw's with a set of barely used clubs.

So for $3 a month for 12 months, a grand total of $36, I became the very proud owner of a barely used set of Sam Snead Blue Ridge clubs with a green plaid canvas bag. Somehow, a used brass blade putter, whose grip required some black friction tape to secure it, was thrown into the deal. Having received a raise for one year of employment at the Weatherford, now earning $1.10 per hour, I felt I could afford this luxury. I played those clubs until the mid 1970's.

In fact, as I think on it, I have only owned three sets of clubs in my entire life. I now play the Nicklaus' I acquired in the late 1980's to replace a set of Hogan blades my brother, James, gave me. The blades were in the trunk of my car when it was stolen. The car was recovered; the blades were not.

I would play at odd hours when green fees were at their lowest. A stanchly committed elderly professional named Bill now ran the golf club. We soon established a barter system that benefited both of us: good used balls for rounds of golf.

Balls were out of my price range, so I hunted for lost balls. A really nice black or red Titliest could be traded to Bill for two weekend rounds. I saved some decent balls for my own play. Bill could sell all of the Titliest, Maxflis, or Wilson Staffs I might find. After the tournament on the July 4th weekend, I never paid another green fee. I had my regular paths I walked early on Sunday and Monday mornings.

Most of these mornings, I would arouse David from his crib and we would go hunt golf balls. I knew the "sweet spots," so to speak. With David on my shoulders, we would make our way through the pine trees and search for balls. On this particular morning, we were in the ponderosa stand that bordered the right side of Number One fairway. Number One was a severe dogleg left that progressively narrowed into the landing area, requiring a nice placement of the tee shot. The result was many balls drifting into the pines to the right.

The golf course was a good place to make friends and to repair friendships. This morning, the left-handed golfing Coach Herb Gregg, playing alone, fored us and teed off.

My relationship with Coach Gregg had been strained since I had left the team as our pregnancy with Mike developed and I felt I needed to work. I regretted the impaired relationship because I really liked the man, and I had learned much from him. Regardless, I moved toward the edge of the fairway as we walked toward each other.

I sat David down and he promptly retrieved Coach Gregg's tee shot from near the base of a tree, held it up for him to see and

Billie and the Boys

ran toward him carrying the ball. The delighted David quickly covered the 15 yards or so. He then handed Coach his ball. Coach laughed, talked to David and took him by the hand. They walked toward me.

We spoke briefly and pleasantly as he continued to hold David's hand. He inquired of the infant Mike. Coach dropped his ball and hit his second shot.

He returned his club to a small canvas bag, turned to me and said, "Come by the gym sometime." He rubbed David's head and added, "He is good boy." We shook hands. The handshake was firm, his nod approving.

I thanked him. He nodded again, smiled and went about his round. I lifted David back onto my shoulders, and we continued our treasure hunt.

Coach Herb Gregg is a good man.

Golf is just a game, but it is a fine game.

CHAPTER FIFTEEN

Summer Visitors

The summer again brought visitors from the east. Mother and Dad returned for a more extended viewing of the new baby.

Aunt Vivian and Uncle Hubert had ridden out with them. Their eldest son, Boots, and his wife, Jackie, were coming to take them to their home in Casa Grande. They were staying the night in a motel just off campus until Boots and Jackie could retrieve them. Recognizing the beautiful view he had of the peaks from their motel, Herb slipped on a sweater to keep off the chill of the Flagstaff morning and took his morning coffee and Roi Tan cigar to the pool. The cool morning air deceived him as to the intensity of the sun in the thin air.

Uncle Hubert dozed. The sun did what the mountain sun does. By the time Boots and Jackie arrived, Uncle was already aware that the top of his bald head was quite burned.

The experience made an impression on him. For years, he enjoyed telling the story of his head getting sunburned while he was wearing a sweater to keep warm. Billie, our granddaughter Emily Ann, and I visited him in a nursing home in Sapulpa, Oklahoma shortly before his death in April of 1990. The ninety five year old Hubert Claunts remembered his blistered head and was still joking about his adventure with the Arizona morning sun.

Annice and Jay, wanting their children to see the Grand Canyon, made the trek west. Their youngest daughter, Barbara Ann, was close to David's age. Freddie and Karen Sue were just older.

Annice bounced out of their green and silver Chevrolet Belaire station wagon and pronounced, "Well! Hal McBride, you – are – lucky!"

Billie and the Boys

She then recounted her fantasies of injuring and maiming me as she gazed out the passenger's window at the barren landscape dotted with roadside signs proclaiming last water for 5 million miles. A long stretch of road broken only by towns she judged to be uninhabitable. She held Gallup, Holbrook, and Winslow in very low regard. She couldn't believe I had brought her baby sister to such a god-forsaken place.

Then as Route 66 brought her closer to Flagstaff, she saw the San Francisco Peaks on the horizon. The junipers and then the pines begin dot the roadside with a steadily increasing density as she approached Flagstaff. With these sights, Annice's mood became increasingly temperate. By her arrival, she had concluded this slash of northern Arizona was not only habitable but was indeed an attractive place.

They stayed with us two nights, sandwiched around a trip to the Grand Canyon. While I just barely knew them, Billie was utterly thrilled to have a sister visiting.

Trains and railroad tracks seemed to give Flagstaff a vibrant and beating heart. Publicized as the fastest passenger train in the United States, The Super Chief would dash into Flagstaff on its route to or from Los Angles. It was a marvelous train.

The tracks gave the illusion of dividing the community into north and south, the commercial downtown to the north and the university to the south. Passenger trains and freight trains came regularly and often. Waiting for a train to clear the crossing at Beaver Street or San Francisco Street was commonplace.

It was such a regular sensory experience that a passing train stimulated the infant Mike far better than any crib mobile. David's early vocabulary included his personalized collection of railroad terminology. We watched the "'rain" pass on the "red-roid-rack" while waiting for the appearance of the "rick-a-boose." Much as we would later watch airplanes arrive and depart from Tulsa International Airport, we would enjoy watching the trains pass. It was both entertaining and inexpensive.

Our boys loved the trains. Their daddy rather liked them too.

CHAPTER SIXTEEN

Northeraire

I was agreeably into summer at the Weatherford when an opportunity came. Dick Grey, the General Manager of Northernaire County Club, a new resort and housing development underway south of Flagstaff in Munds Park, offered me a job at $2.20 an hour. This amount was exactly double what I was making at the Weatherford. The hours were to be eight to four with Monday and Tuesday off. He said there would soon be transportation provided. As much as I liked my job at the Weatherford, I didn't feel I could decline such an offer.

Our Cottage City neighbor Paul Lansing, who was now working the graveyard shift at the Weatherford, was willing and capable of taking over the front desk.

Billie was on unpaid maternity leave from Mountain States. We had two children. We needed the money.

Northernaire was envisioned as an elite mountain resort. More than an escape from the searing heat of the deserts of southern Arizona, it was to be an Arizona mountain refuge from the heat and humidity of the large cities of the upper Midwest. An Augusta National located in the mountains of northern Arizona.

The club house with its dining room and bar were by far the most elegant places I had ever seen. There were guest houses on the property with views of the golf course and homes being built on the tree filled hillside that rose from Munds Park to the north.

The Black Canyon highway, now I-17, was under construction and bordered the property to the west. The only access to the property was by an unpaved county road out of Flagstaff. You drove on what became little more than a dirt trail, possibly a Forest Service road, until you intersected the Black Canyon highway. Not yet really a highway, it was an elongated gash of construction that changed its route almost daily. You

Billie and the Boys

dodged huge clods of dirt, pot holes, and freshly upturned boulders. The heavy road construction equipment whose operators viewed most automobiles as intruders on the roadway seemed to go out of their way to make your passage difficult.

Employees living in the Verde valley came from the south and followed the twisting path of the gravel road out of Sedona and up Schnebly Hill, shortening their distance in the construction zone. With either route, you ultimately drove on this ever-changing washboard of a road bed. No, a washboard has some regularity to it. This road was an evolving obstacle course, redesigned daily and intent upon doing harm to you and your car.

As much as I had come to enjoy the Weatherford, I came to dislike Northernaire. While my income did more than double my Weatherford Hotel wages, I found Dick Grey to be a less than honorable man. The bus-like vehicle that was supposed to provide transport from Flagstaff on July 1 never materialized, so I was driving our Plymouth to the property, leaving Billie alone with the boys some ten rough, rutted miles away. I would get home after midnight. I was learning the painful lesson that there would be times in life that money just wasn't as important as it might have seemed.

Then, when I didn't think it could get any worse, the monsoon rains arrived. They would build off the rim, rising to drench Munds Park with violent afternoon thunderstorms. These storms could leave the construction zone impassible, often for days at a time. If I couldn't get to the property, I didn't get paid. If I was at the property, I couldn't get back home, leaving Billie and the boys alone and without transportation. We endured this for two and a half months.

From my prospective, the only positive things to come from my employment this rainy northern Arizona summer was that I was given the chance to become acquainted with two men I would have ever come to know them otherwise. Truth be told, it is unlikely I would have had the opportunity to ever meet either of these men, much less come to know them.

During these evenings when we were stranded on the property, we played knock poker on the floor of an empty and unfurnished room next to the front desk. The bar manager, the golf pro Fielding Abbott, his assistant, the tennis pro and me were the regulars.

Barry Goldwater, one of the United States Senators from Arizona, was a regular guest at Northernaire. He heard of the poker games. One evening, he simply arrived with several rolls of nickels in his hand and asked to join us. He seated himself on the floor, folded up his legs beneath him and broke open his nickels.

I believe the Senator enjoyed the games as much as any of us. He competed for every nickel but never treated losing as if was a disaster, hooted at the off-color jokes and often made fun of his exaggerated frailties.

Given my position at the desk, I had already told Billie of the kind and respectful manner in which he treated his wife, Peggy, while she struggled with issues of her own. On those evenings, he approached her with an extraordinary gentleness and sensitivity.

Soon I think just killing time before the game would begin, the Senator started to pull a chair from the bar into the generous space I occupied behind the front desk. I frankly didn't know the importance of this man and his family to the State of Arizona. My naive lack of preconception concerning his status might well have been why he seemed to enjoy our conversations.

He was curious about eastern Oklahoma and Stigler but he was especially interested in my impressions of Arizona. One evening I told him of my car buying excursion to Phoenix and the drive back to Flagstaff to him. My recollections of the drive seemed to provide him with considerable satisfaction. His love of his native state was infinite.

He liked that I could discuss rather obscure sites in northern Arizona. I confessed I had acquired much of it from Forest Service maps while passing the late nights at the Weatherford Hotel and from Billie's experiences at Mountain States, connecting people to telephones located in remote trading post on the Navajo and Hopi reservations.

We spoke of my grandfather.

I was captivated by his accounts of his trips into the Grand Canyon and his tales of the reservations. He possessed an unrestrained eagerness to share his knowledge of the Hopi

Billie and the Boys

religion and the Kachina doll. He admired the ethical foundation woven into the entire fabric of the Hopi life.

I believe I will always aspire to be as impassioned in my love of place as this then 50 year old native son of Arizona. He spoke so eloquently, yet in the most simple of terms, he talked of the land and his beliefs; he endeavored to understand as if the land itself had a voice.

The lines of his face and the sun-marked ruddiness of his complexion gave away a long and immense familiarity with the outdoors that most would never enjoy.

My sons have repeatedly accused me of voting for Senator Goldwater just so I could say I played poker with the President of the United States. In the 1964 Presidential election, Billie and I stood in line a considerable length of time, marked our ballots and cancelled each other's vote.

Thorne Donnelley, retired from a family printing and publishing business, after some disagreement the bar staff about his placing the bottle of Lancers he would bring from his home in their chiller, he stomped past me and placed it the refrigerator in the small room behind the front desk. His round of golf completed, he retrieved his bottle of Lancers, produced a cork screw and went to the dining room for lunch.

The next morning I saw him coming. I extended my hand. He gave me the bottle of Lancers and I placed it in the refrigerator. After a time, he appeared with two sandwiches from the dining room. He would sit behind the desk. We would eat and talk, no, he would talk and I would listen, while he downed his large bottle of quality rosé.

He would give elaborate accounts of his exotic hunts. After a time, he said, "I expand things a bit." It didn't matter his stories were just uncomplicated fun.

At this time of his life his real passion seemed to be his elephant rifles. More precisely, he loved enticing an unsuspecting Northernaire guest to come to his home on top of the hill to north of the clubhouse, to come and experience the thrill of firing one of his very large caliber elephant rifles on the range he had constructed behind his home.

After sipping a couple of his alcohol laden sweet concoctions and firing one of his rifles, the most experience hunter's shoulder would be far too sore to make a respectable golf swing the next day. Often there would be a wager and a round of golf scheduled with their most congenital host the next morning.

He told great stories of people I know I should have known, but didn't. My lack of knowledge made his stories none the less grand.

Thorne Donnelley was every inch the leprechaun.

The first of August, Billie wanted to go back to Oklahoma for a few weeks. Mother and Dad met us in Albuquerque. I worked two more weeks before quitting the job at Northernaire.

Senator Goldwater was on the property at the time and sought me out. He offered to find me a job somewhere in his stores in Phoenix. While it might have been a good move, it didn't seem so at the moment.

He said he understood why I might want to remain in the mountain country. He made a telephone call to the Babbitt's in Flagstaff. They immediately offered me a position at the store in Williams until something was available in Flagstaff. After a brief telephone conversation with Billie, I declined the position and remained committed to staying in school.

I admired Senator Goldwater. Although I never saw him after that summer, I felt a sense of loss when this gracious man died in 1998.

I had bent a tie-rod on the Plymouth during my commutes over the treacherous, rutted construction zone, the final straw coming when a piece of heavy equipment forced the Plymouth into an exotic and unexplored segment of the roadbed. A charitable mechanic at Northernaire straightened and strengthened the tie-rod with a welding torch. He seemed to employ the same instruments and techniques used to keep the tractor fleet running on the grounds.

I went to get Billie and the boys. The Plymouth and I made a quick trip to Stigler, returning to Flagstaff just before Billie's maternity leave with Mountain States expired.

CHAPTER SEVENTEEN

H & H Wholesale

Back in Flagstaff, enrolled but unemployed, I went to visit Coach Spilsbury. He made a telephone call to the campus employment office. He handed me a slip of paper with the names and telephone numbers for two openings.

Bypassing the telephone, I went directly to H & H Wholesale. Ralph Hubert interviewed and hired me. I began work the next day.

H & H Wholesale was owned and operated by Ralph Hubert and Arnold Herrera. Both had been employees of Arizona Foods in Phoenix, Arnold in sales and Ralph as warehouse supervisor, before venturing out in their own business in the early 1950's. Arnold was responsible for sales and Ralph ran the warehouse.

H & H Wholesale, a wholesale grocer, primarily supplying restaurants in Flagstaff, Winslow, Holbrook, Williams, and a variety of restaurants and trading post on the Navajo Reservation.

It was a modest but efficient and profitable operation. There were two full-time warehouse men when I started who made the delivery runs to the customers. One left after I been there only a week.

My job was in the warehouse, filling orders and loading trucks. I worked from 1 to 5 weekdays and 8 to 12 on Saturday for $1.75 an hour.

Ralph Hubert, who I judged to be in his late 50's, was a short balding man with a slight paunch, a reddish complexion and a cigar that seemed a part of his physical makeup. In both appearance and demeanor, he reminded me a great deal of my uncle, Hubert Claunts. Ralph had a similar pride in his warehouse to that my uncle and my grandfather had their Stigler stores, right down to seeing that it was swept and organized before he left for the night.

Ralph viewed his warehouse as a living breathing organism with his fork-lift its primary appendage. He drove an aging three wheeled gasoline powered fork-lift that had been painted navy blue at one time, but the paint was flaking off in a number of places leaving the metal exposed. The operator stood on a platform, a steering wheel with a knob to his right hand side, speed was controlled by foot treadle while levers to the left of the steering wheel raised and lowered the blades. Ralph would spin that lift around and race from location to location as I stacked the merchandise on the pallet. The warehouse would fill with the fumes from the exhaust.

The man was very territorial about his fork-lift. Beyond that he would willingly teach me every nuance of the warehouse.

Arnold Herrera, seemingly much younger than Ralph, was of Mexican descent with a sharp angular structure to his face. He had the ready laugh and quick smile of the good salesman. Since his responsibility was mostly in the office or on the road, I rarely saw him during those early months.

With two sons, 4 months old and 22 months old, Billie was back at the telephone company. She was finding being away from the boys increasingly distasteful.

I was taking a full load packed into a Monday-Wednesday-Friday schedule at ASC and working part time. We managed our schedule in such a manner that the boys were with one of us all but 2 or 3 half-days each week. Getting a job that allowed me to be home in the evenings was satisfying. I felt fortune to have gotten this job.

The summer season was passing and the partners decided they could get along with one full time driver and just me to assist Ralph in the warehouse. So, Arnold secured the orders, Ralph filled the orders, the driver delivered the orders.

I don't recall the details but something changed. Having no classes on Tuesday or Thursday, I began to make the delivery on the Holbrook-Winslow route and the every other Tuesday deliveries to the Navajo Reservation.

Billie and the Boys

H & H provided me with the opportunity to see places in northern Arizona I would never have otherwise visited. The restaurant owners were diverse group ranging from a Greek immigrant who took me under his wing to the owners of Chinese descent who seemed less eager to trust.

There was a normalcy to our family schedule. The blend of classes and work now allowed me to be home each evening. Most days that meant dinner with Billie and the boys, helping bathe the boys and reading to them at bedtime, and finishing the day with Billie on the couch watching our little Crosley television. It seemed a comfortable blueprint for a normal life.

I liked it.

I don't remember when either of our sons took his first trip to a gym or watched a basketball game, but suffice it to say they were extremely young. So, the concept of tossing a ball toward a basket was never really foreign to them. During their visit during summer of 1959, Dad had bought David a ball at the Stigler 5 & Up. It was clear plastic with colored dots the size of a nickel, and he adored it. We rolled the ball in the floor. Then, he began to place the ball through the basket I made with by arms. Shortly he began to shoot the ball, first through my arms advancing to a hoop made of wire coat hanger. Ultimately I made a net of green yarn for the hanger and placed it over the front door. David fired away.

I believe it is plausible to assume that neither of our boys can recall a time when they didn't know how to shoot a basketball or throw a baseball.

CHAPTER EIGHTEEN

The Reservation

My first established sales route was both a delivery route and a sales route north out of Flagstaff to the reservations. Orders were delivered and orders were taken for two weeks later. I really looked forward to this. The Navajo Reservation was a completely foreign world. Ralph talked with me before my first reservation venture about the nature of Tribal law and that only Tribal law existed on the reservation. He perceived it as historically harsh with outsiders who violated the traffic laws. His cautionary tales only further intrigued me.

The route gave me the opportunity to see places that I had heard of during my time at the Weatherford Hotel and communities whose names Billie had taught me to pronounce from her work at the telephone company.

I liked to leave very early and driving to the furthest delivery point during the early morning hours, working my way back.

Billie and the Boys

Daybreak would find me on Hiway 89 well north of the exit to Tuba City. In the beginning I didn't know quite what to make of a landscape dominated by an immeasurable emptiness. That this was the most barren, desolate place I had ever been was my first impression. By comparison, it made the desert around Phoenix lush.

The Navajo Bridge spanned the Colorado River and the depth of the canyon it spanned surprised me. As a flatlander, I had considered the walls of Oak Creek Canyon to be steep. The sheer drop of the canyon wall descending to a river so far below was startling.

In one sense I am uncertain that I ever developed a great affection for this vast unforgiving land to the north of Flagstaff. I am convinced that I ever encountered a landscape that makes you more reflective and ultimately demands that it be approached with a philosophical reverence.

I never believed you could drive miles and miles of a state hiway, winding along buttes, dry washes and residual mountains and never encounter another vehicle. But in 1959 you could.

From my late evening conversations with the men of Merritt, Chapman and Scott in the lobby of Weatherford I should have known this would change as surely as they were tunneling through the walls of the Glen Canyon so that the Colorado River could be diverted allowing the construction of a dam to northeast of Bitter Springs.

Today streams of cars drawn by the recreational promise of Lake Powell crowd this hiway. It is anything but unoccupied.

The northernmost point of my route was a trading post near Vermillion Cliffs. It was constructed from the red native stone that surrounded it, a long narrow building that blended so well with its physical environment that it could be passed almost unnoticed despite the single gas pump not far from the roadbed.

The man who owned the trading post appeared to have stepped from the screen of a John Wayne movie. A stark slender wind burned man always dressed in a chambray cowboy shirt, denim jeans and a large but not gaudy tortoise belt. The dust seemed to seek him out and cling to him. There was a true ambivalence to the man, quite amiable yet as inhospitable as the land that framed his trading post. He was very direct; he wanted what he wanted, no more, no less.

He offered me coffee, drank from metal cups coated with blue enamel and made in a metal coffee pot. Clean is not an adjective I would choose for either. I remember the coffee as being good.

Regardless of the weather, we sat on a dirt floored porch in wooden, cane bottomed chairs facing west and watched the lines of light from sun as it cleared the cliffs behind us striking the buttes to the west

Conversation was limited. If there was something he wanted me to take note of, he would most often simply point to it. He was only interested in what I might have seen on my trip up. While most I would come to know on the reservation route were only seeking a way to escape to a more civilized setting, he seemed completely at ease with his place.

I always filled the gas tank of the bobtail truck at Vermillion Cliffs Trading Post.

I cannot remember his name, but I will never forget the man.

Tuba City was the most populated stop on this route. There was a passable café with little to recommend it. The owner was always cordial. What I recall most about the Tuba City Café was how they fried eggs, cracked directly into a deep fat fryer and cooked until they floated. No surprise they bought as many sixty pound tins of shortening as any restaurant I would ever service.

Tuba City was marked by its base poverty. Many still lived in hogans which appeared as mounds of the pale rusty reddish-orange soil covering an endoskeleton made from juniper and pinion pine, a smoke hole in middle and a single light bulb hanging outside. To forget the first time you see meat, being jerked on an open air rack, thinly sliced and periodically salted, regularly turned toward the sun to scatter the flies that collected on the shady side, would be a challenge.

Just to the south of Tuba City was a seemingly oddly placed Hopi village, Lower Moencopi. I recall it as setting in a valley seeming to be more distant from Tuba City than it actually was. The road sloped down into the settlement.

It was a Hopi island surrounded by Navajo lands. An attempt was made to explain its existence to me along with an explanation as to why the only water had to come from a sacred source. If I ever understood the logic it has long since escaped me.

Like the trading post at Vermillion Cliffs, the little community appeared to be at peace with its surroundings. Every structure in Lower Moencopi appeared to be the same soft sand sun-bleached adobe. It took little imagination to believe the buildings had simply sprouted from the earth.

On warm days I would buy a very cold grape soda from our small account there. Any purchase I made seemed to please the Hopi family who operated the store.

It was my next to the last stop and I was rarely in a great rush to leave Lower Moencopi. I felt there was an indefinable and almost mystical quality to this place.

Cameron was my final stop. With its hotel, restaurant, trading post and gift shop, Cameron catered to people desiring to use the eastern entry to the Grand Canyon. Its southwestern architecture belied its fine dining room with cloth napkins. I always intended to come back some day and stay in the rustic hotel there. I never did, at least I haven't yet.

This route would eventually bring me to Page. From my time at the Weatherford Hotel and tales of the Merritt, Chapman and Scott men, I had visions of this primate outpost sitting on the edge of nowhere. The Page of 1959 did nothing to tarnish that illusion.

After departing the hiway at Bitter Springs, the road to Page was virtually primordial following a path of least resistance, a route dictated by the land itself. The road was mostly graded with tiny sections of asphalt promising better things to come. There were semi-official traffic indicators staked beside the roadway providing a general direction that was to be followed.

Page was actually a tent city at the time. I don't believe there was anything that would pass for a permanent structure. It was just tents, many of them quite large, erected near the canyon wall. The Glen Canyon Bridge spanning the canyon had recently been completed.

I delivered a grocery order, mostly canned goods, to the cafeteria that served the Merritt, Chapman and Scott employees.

By contacting one of the men who had stayed so many weekends at the Weatherford, I got a closer view of the canyon walls and the diversion tunnels than I ever anticipated.

I has given a steel hat and guided onto an open air elevator floored with wooden beams. I was uncomfortable just stepping from the solid ground onto the elevator suspended over the canyon. The elevator swaying in breezes of the canyon did nothing to enhance my fraying sense of security. The squeaking noises that seemed to come from the cable and the increasing side to side movement as we began the descent was not reassuring.

Despite the distraction of uncomplicated apprehension, just plain old fear, the sights from this open air elevator dropping us down, on occasion tapping against the sheer rock walls, and onto the floor of the Glen Canyon were visually extravagant. It is only with this writing that I increasingly realizing how much of northern Arizona is just that visually extravagant.

I am certain I would have enjoyed the ride even more had the wobbly wooden floored elevator provided any sense of security and if I was not preoccupied with concealing my fear from my seasoned companions. Companions whom I suspect were obtaining considerable pleasure from watching me take their regular commute to the bottom of the canyon.

At times it did seem that the "Glen Canyon Trolley" was going to wildly descend, smashing on the canyon floor.

I briefly felt some better when after the tour when Malley, a round red-faced Irishman and a Weatherford regular, said I had done considerably better that the Federal Inspector who had ridden "Glen's trolley" a couple of weeks earlier. With a proper pace and completely dry delivery he partially retracted what I had taken to be a compliment, saying "Peed his pants".

In a number of classes over the years, I would use this experience as an example of counter-phobia, more fearful of being considered fearful than you are of the actual source of your fear.

Billie and I drove the boys to Page during the summer of 1960. The appearance of the city had not yet taken on any tangible sense of permanence. The waters of the diverted Colorado River were now roaring through the completed tunnels. My acquaintances were off to some other job site in some other part of the world. Other men were preparing to erect the dam itself.

Our money was always short. My Uncle Howett on a couple of occasions sent a five dollar bill with a note saying buy a hamburger. It never went to buying a hamburger. I recall once paying Howett's five dollars on the Meadow Gold milk bill. The Meadow Gold driver carried a large part of Cottage City on a monthly credit, often waiting until some check from somewhere or another arrived.

After I began working for H & H several customers gave us substantial discounts. A great burger place that remains in business, Miz Zip's, was especially generous. The free child's root beers at the A&W were big hits as well.

There came a time in deep fall of 1959 that the well noted "butter for beans swap" occurred. One of the perks of working for H & H was that you got the extra beans. Pinto and lima beans were re-bagged from one hundred pound bags into ten pound bags for resale. There was always an overage of five to seven pounds of beans each time. I did the re-packaging in the warehouse, so I got the beans.

Paul and Brownie Lansing, both not long out of the Navy, were living in next door to Connie and Lamar's unit. They had rapidly become very close friends. Somehow they had acquired an excess of butter. Butter was important to Billie. Billie would always say, "If we ever get the money, I'll never use margarine again". By the time we had the money some researcher had concluded butter was "not heart healthy".

We had beans; Paul and Brownie had butter. I don't recall the exact quantities of the swap, but while Meadow Gold would continue to deliver milk and eggs to our doors, we were both otherwise without food. With a payday some distance away, we swapped beans for butter.

For a number of Christmases, a Gerber's baby food jar filled with lima beans made its way between our homes.

David and Michael got the chicken pox. David had it first and his case was very mild.

Michael's was severe. He broke out every place an infant can break out. We tried lotions and soaks, salves and love, but nothing soothed him. The disease ran its course, the open oozing sores scabbed and then healed. Michael weathered the disease unscarred, but the scar it left with me was a loss of belief. I had a frontal encounter with a variable of life that I did not manage well. While I do recognize the relative status of Chicken Pox in the overall scheme of diseases, I did not like my child being so ill. Billie did better.

The story is "Granny Bam" Lell lived across the street from Ezra and Mary Martin and their daughters in Vian. Granny Bam had simply seen too many children die during her lifetime. She is said to have put forth a resolute and heroic effort to see that the new infant girl in the Martin household survived the whooping cough.

Granny Bam took the infant Billie into her home so the disease didn't spread to the other children. There with a concoction comprised of kerosene, honey and concern she nursed Billie toward health. She devised a screen of blankets that hung from a rope screening the sick bed. While Lou and Annice would come and go, pressing their noses again the closest window to catch a glimpse of the goings on, it was Pauline who stood a doorway vigil as Granny Bam cared for the infant.

During the third week the rattling coughing spasms diminished and the fever broke. The baby girl survived the illness.

With her deeper understanding that children get well and that in the larger scheme of things the chicken pox wasn't so bad, Billie managed the ill child thing better than I did. She still does.

Billie and the Boys

In its wake, the boys' bout with chicken pox left me with a restructured mindset. Our schedules seemed unrelenting. I sensed that formal education was headed for a hiatus. The mental winds of responsibility had shifted. Billie and I needed a reprieve.

CHAPTER NINETEEN

Gone to Town

As the fall semester was coming to a close, Ralph Herbert had been diagnosed with cancer for about a month. His treatment now increasingly took him away from the business, Ralph and Arnold approached me with the offer of a full time job. Still owing money on my fall semester tuition and with no windfall in sight, the prospect for a spring enrollment was dim. The strain of balancing an ever shifting weight atop a three legged stool made the seemingly substantial monthly salary and the use of a pickup truck sound quite attractive. Above all else, it held the promise of what seemed to be a normal life for Billie and the boys.

In January of 1960, I accepted their offer. We moved from Cottage City and into a house in east Flagstaff on Patterson Drive.

Billie bought white Naugahyde couch and matching chair, a second chair with wooden arms and orange Naugahyde seat and back. a coffee table with a matching step table, a chrome dinette set, and a complete bedroom set. The amazing thing is that somehow the payment on this furniture was well within our budget.

In the boys' bedroom were the twin beds James and I had slept in. I liked that.

Billie and the Boys

About a month later we received a telephone that James and Wilma were headed our way with their infant daughter, Shari Lynn. I still don't know exactly why they decided to move to Flagstaff but I was very glad they were coming.

They stayed with us for a few days. Wilma located a nice one bedroom house. James found a job at a service station in downtown on Route 66. I don't remember if it was her first job in Flagstaff, but Wilma soon found a job in the office at Cheshire Chevrolet.

There was a major July 4th fringe benefit to Wilma's new job. We had access to a rooftop from which to view the Pow-Wow parades. As I have said, we really enjoyed Pow-Wow.

We had been on Patterson about four months when our landlords, a divorcing couple, reconciled and wanted to return to their home. The amount of the rent was straining our budget so their decision was not entirely unwelcome.

James and Wilma had now rented a larger house in Pine Knoll with a level grassy back yard. We found a house about a block and a half from them. Billie and I moved to 124 Paseo Del Flag.

The house needed considerable cleaning. Again, I was amazed at Billie's talents with a house. Within days, it appeared every piece of furniture fit like it had been designed for this house.

It was the lot that made this house unique. The back yard had a sharp incline beginning just paces beyond the backdoor that elevated the yard into a dense grove of pines. The drive way in front sloped upward to the house which sat well above street level. There was a large pine and two smaller pines in the front yard.

The view of the San Francisco Peaks from the living room and front bedroom was as fine as Flagstaff had to offer. While I enjoyed the open windows in our Cottage City bedroom, this was unbelievable. Drowsy, lying beneath the quilts in the chilly breeze of summer mornings on Pine Knoll created an indelible memory.

James and Wilma's house just west of us had a great privacy fence to go with that blue grass back yard became the site of something resembling a baseball game. A plastic baseball bat and something like a wiffle ball were purchased. James and I had great fun pitching to David who would hit the ball then make a mad sliding dash to some designated base.

Mike just wanted to run and slide anywhere. Early in the summer of 1960 his slides at time were a bit awkward and ill-timed, more head first tumbles than slides. By summer's end, he was taking his turn swinging for the fences, then dashing toward the base.

Much to the boys' chagrin, by fall Shari was crawling into the base paths. Her daddy encouraged her. She seemed to love every second of it.

Flagstaff winters are long but the five months between are luxurious. At 6900 feet daylight lingers late into the evening, no one wanted to be inside. While many evenings were spent in James and Wilma's yard, there were also late afternoon picnics in city parks seemingly filled with children. On the weekends, we cooked out a Lake Mary or ate our lunches on the banks of Oak Creek.

I was glad James and Wilma had decided to move to Flagstaff. Billie and I enjoyed them.

Some way I found the time to play golf in the early daylight of summer. There was no dew to scrape on a Flagstaff morning.

Come fall, James hunted although he had not been in Arizona long enough to obtain a valid hunting license. I cautioned him, but he seemed to believe that all game wardens were as caring and understanding as Bill Clement had been. They weren't.

I have forgotten the amount of the fine for hunting deer without a license, but James paid one. I never heard him complain about the fine. It was almost "Well, you caught me fair and square." He did complain long and loud about the one year suspension from hunting or fishing in Arizona.

Ralph Herbert's cancer was increasingly disabling him, most days he was only at the warehouse briefly if at all. The summer season was approaching and business had been increasing. It was evident that another employee was needed at H & H Wholesale. James was hired and for about a year and a half I got to work beside my brother.

James made the deliveries of my Monday and Wednesday sales. On Tuesday and Thursday, we put the orders together and loaded them into the truck. I believe we both really enjoyed our time together at H & H. We worked hard and had a good time doing it. We both gained a working knowledge of the wholesale grocery business that would benefit us several times over the coming years.

As part of our Winslow route, we serviced the City Jail. I suppose indicative of future predilections James would take his lunch and visit at the Winslow Police Department. He enjoyed company of the policemen.

With the required Forest Service permits in hand, James and I took the boys to secure Christmas trees. Billie issued cautionary advice about cutting a tree of appropriate size for the living rooms. More by good fortune than by good judgment, the selected tree was a perfect fit.

As would become our longstanding tradition, I strung the lights and Billie placed the ornaments with Christmas care. This was truly beautiful tree. From the road, you could look up pass the pines and see the tree.

Mike was twenty months old and he thought it more than beautiful. He must have felt it had some ethereal property to it. He looked at it silence for several minutes. Then, he charged the tree and with one great leap landed in the middle of the tree. The Glass ornaments crashed and shattered as the tree collided with the floor.

Mike, partly sitting and partly lying but completely engulfed in a festive laughter, was in the middle of it all. The blithe little spirit of the season had landed.

After reinstructing Mike and resurrecting the tree a couple of times, Mike would take his pointing finger and touch ball dangling from the lowered branches, each contact increasing the motion of the ball until it would fall, shattering at the dancing feet of a little boy.

By day's end, all the ornaments had been removed from the lower branches. Billie and I thought we had reached an acceptable compromise with our youngest, a tree truce so to speak. We believed that until we heard the tree crash to the floor again.

Billie decided the best solution was to acknowledge that the tree was there for the boys. Mike enjoyed the tree. "Timber!!!"

Although I was rooting for her hold on for six more days, Wilma delivered Sandy Lee on February 16, 1961. I still blame a meal of Mexican food at Morales Diner for her early arrival.

CHAPTER TWENTY

Jimmy the Greek

Some customers were unique unto themselves. On the west end of Winslow was a small white wood frame café. Even though freshly painted each spring, the sun and wind had so treated the wood that the building always seemed to look as if it were always in need of a coat of paint. The structure's appearance resembled that of its owner, weathered and worn but sturdy and stable.

Whatever the appearance of the structure, it was not the result of a lack of pride on the part of the ownership. No man was ever prouder of his business than Jimmy. His little café did a brisk local business that completely belied the business's crusty exterior.

I wish I could recall his last name but I can't. And even then when I kind of knew it, I could not pronounce it. He once at my insistence made a brief effort to help me pronounce it correctly. He became exasperated. I was mystified by the sounds I couldn't quite get my tongue around. He said Jimmy would do. It was all anyone ever called him and it was what I called him when we spoke.

In telling Billie about him, I would call him Jimmy the Greek.

Jimmy had immigrated to the United States from Greece as a very young man. Even though he was unable to speak a word of English upon his arrival, he worked many jobs from dock hand to dishwasher. He would say he liked the restaurants because with those jobs he was always certain of a meal.

He followed the railroads until they led him to Winslow during the Great Depression. He had diligently saved his money. When the man for whom he was working as a fry cook decided to give up the business, Jimmy bought it. I cannot explain how much this café represented America's dream to her adopted son.

Jimmy was proud of his café and its products. From his grill, he fashioned hamburgers smothered in onions and cheese. Hot dogs became coneys covered with melted cheese, chili, and sweet relish. Large pots simmered on a stove in the back room. Jimmy served chili with grease that floated to the top, white beans to be served with a sinus clearing dose of an enhanced Tabasco sauce and a thick beef stew made from whatever was fresh and available. There were ice cold bottles of Coca-Cola to wash down the delicacy of your choice.

Jimmy's wife, a short, stout-framed woman who spoke few words and shared even fewer thoughts, prepared the tuna salad and pimento cheese for sandwiches.

When I was first given the sales duties, I called on Jimmy in the logical order, at the end of the breakfast business. He would tell me to come back later and then just ignore me. After a few times of coming back later, I asked him when he wanted me to call on him. He said anytime after two o'clock.

While I had known him from my days on the delivery truck, I am not certain when our first genuine conversation occurred, however, it was after I took the sales route that Jimmy and I became friends. We would sit on the cases stacked in the small store room. He talked about his business and about this country. While he was proud of his Greek heritage, he was so enraptured with his United States citizenship that a simple political discussion would become impassioned, so stimulating him that you had no doubts of his absolute allegiance to our country. He had limited tolerance for those he perceived as being disrespectful. Not voting was a mortal sin, as voting was a sacred obligation.

You never left one of these discussions, often more position presentation than dialogue, without a real grasp of how grateful this man was to the country that had opened its doors to him. He loved being an American and being a businessman.

At times, I would tell him that my grandfather would say that an unlocked door is useful only if a man chooses to open it and walk through. He liked that idea.

This feisty little Greek man spent his life walking through doors others might have viewed as closed. He was not timid in the face of the unfamiliar.

We would visit and I would take his order. He was my favorite stop. He always had a joke that he had been saving to tell me. The jokes were often corny, but he so enjoyed telling them.

Jimmy's cafe was my last stop before heading for Flagstaff. One July afternoon, not far from Winslow, I noticed the sky to the west had become an orange-brown and seemed to be rolling toward me like an Oklahoma thunderstorm.

I had heard of dust storms, especially on the desert floors to the south, but I had ever seen one. It literally does appear to be a solid rock wall with dust rising from its top and undulating toward you; then, it engulfs you.

I was slow to realize what was coming, but when I did I pulled over and got as close to two junipers as I could and turned on the emergency blinkers just as the storm rolled over me. It was like the world become completely brown. The wind violently rocked the relatively new white Ford Econoline pickup and pelted it with what sounded like pebbles. It was louder that Oklahoma hail hitting a tin roof. I felt the odd sensation of the truck being scooted along the ground, but my logic dictated that it could not be happening.

It took me an odd moment to realize the storm had passed because the front window was so pitted that it looked to be a pane of frosted glass. A trucker who had pulled over behind me honked. I opened the door. My truck had been pushed away from the junipers and the truck bed was just edging onto the highway. The trucker shielded me until I could move the pickup back to the side of the road.

The storm had sandblasted the entire front of the truck. The paint had been totally removed. There was not even the tiniest of openings remaining that would allow me to see through the windshield.

I considered my situation and made my decision. With my head leaning out the window, I drove into Flagstaff. By the time I arrived at the warehouse, Jimmy realizing the severity of the storm, had called to check on my safe arrival. His concern could not have been more genuine.

Jimmy was one of the most contented men I had ever known. That is the way he was right up until the day the doctor told him his chronic indigestion was cancer -- cancer now so advanced that the medicine of 1961 could do nothing to assist him.

At first, it was his intention to simply cook his way into eternity. A few weeks later, saying "Since your from Oklahoma," he asked me what I knew about a healing preacher named Oral Roberts. I had never heard of him. I told him I was skeptical of any tent evangelist. I realize that this bias might have had its origins in my experience with my Mema Lane and the Book of Revelation in a steamy tent in Miami, Oklahoma when I was in the fourth grade.

Over the coming weeks, Jimmy would tell me about listening to him on the radio. Jimmy was coming to believe a healing experience was possible. First, he began to send a little money, then more considerable money to the evangelist.

Within the month, Jimmy bought airline tickets for him and his wife. They were bound for somewhere in the Carolinas. He mortgaged his café and took the money with him. He felt he was taking a pilgrimage to spiritual and physical salvation. He believed he was going to be healed.

My vulnerable friend found the evangelist to be completely mesmerizing. Having been told he was healed in front of a gathering in Carolina, he returned to Winslow and to his café. He was now substantially in debt for the first time in his life but buoyed by the belief he had been healed.

Two weeks later, Jimmy died. I went to his funeral. The café never reopened. Within the month, there was a For Sale sign in front of the building giving contact information for a local bank. His wife had gone to live with her relatives.

The building was still for sale when we left Arizona.

My personal epitaph of him will always read, "Jimmy the Greek a good American."

As I think back on it now, in the larger schemas of relative harm, the evangelist at the Miami tent revival was only scaring small boys.

CHAPTER TWENTY-ONE

Alums

April 8, 1961

In early April of 1961, Coach Spilsbury called in a favor. The Flagstaff Kiwanis Club was putting together a Second Annual Varsity-Alumni Spring game. Coach Spilsbury badly wanted this game to become a tradition at the conclusion to spring practice.

I got a telephone call from Coach. He was to the point. He was concerned there would be a shortage of alums available. He asked me to play. Having not played since high school and having lost any real enthusiasm for the game, I had my doubts.

However, Coach Spilsbury could be persuasive and, without question, I owed him. So, I said reluctantly agreed.

Bill McCormick, a running back on the 1958 team, was organizing the Alums. Bill and his wife, Nancy, had remained in Flagstaff. He was now a salesman for Friend's Sales, a local office supply company. Bill assured me there would be plenty of alums arriving on game day, but, just in case, I needed to be ready to play.

A small group of us were still in Flagstaff, either employed or still in school. I remember Mickey Alzola, Danny Loveall, Cruz Salas, and Pete Kotchow.

Then there was Ray Harris. Ray was either the most masochistic or the toughest soul I knew. He was the center on the 1958 team, and I don't believe he had a disk in his neck or back that wasn't pinched or crushed, but he kept right on playing. I think at this point his wife, Sonja, was trying to finish school. With football done, Ray seemed to be focusing in the healing properties of trout fishing.

He declared himself fit and ready to play. Sonja was the only wife who thought her husband's participation was crazier that Billie considered mine to be. They were both correct as wives are prone to be in such matters.

Though the strongest I had ever been, a workout or two pointed to a woeful lack of conditioning. However, I was committed to not setting foot on the field, so I wasn't too concerned.

Saturday came and a greater than expected number of alums arrived. I breathed even easier.

Even more unexpectedly, our impact player arrived. He was something of a legend before my time. I just wish I could recall his name. For some reason, the name of Hector sticks in my mind, perhaps because of the hero in Greek mythology. For no reason other than identification, Hector it will be here.

He roared in on his motorcycle having ridden from Los Angeles just to play the game. I mean *roared* in. He drove through an open gate and parked his motorcycle between the fence and dressing room entrance, giving the accelerator a couple of extra twists for emphasis. It was whispered in my ear that he had a wide mean streak and simply loved the hitting.

His rough roguish appearance in jeans and boots with his dark black, wild windblown hair, coupled with a sulk that would have done Dean or Brando proud did nothing to belie the reputation. Then, he laughed. Within two hours, I had no question about his love of competition. This was funny kind man who relished projecting the wayward image.

My plan for avoiding play went well until the mid-point of the third quarter when someone came hobbling off. As I was moving away from his exit path, someone grabbed my shoulder pad and said, "Wide side linebacker." Seeing no graceful way out, I stepped on to the field.

Hector was in the middle. I shrugged; he laughed and shoved me into position. The second play came right at me. I still have a crisp mental image of Jim Eis, a solid fullback, coming at me full open. With a collision imminent and appearing unavoidable, I got a step into the gap before we hit. Well, Jim and I collided just before Hector completely leveled both of us.

For a quarter and a half, Hector gave me a tutorial on defensive football. The properties of testosterone merged with adrenaline in the young adult male are a true puzzlement. I believe it is intended to be so.

This hormonal witch's brew, perhaps more properly "warlock's wine," in the older adult male remains equally inexplicable.

Courtesy of George Nackard, we found ice chests of beer in the dressing room along with boxes of sandwiches the school food service had prepared.

After showering, we carried the food and beer into the stands and on a cool April mountain evening, there we sat.

For that single night, Hector was my best friend. We sat in the stands with Bill McCormick, drank beer and told stories – and perhaps an exaggeration of two. Cafeteria ham and cheese sandwiches never tasted so grand.

Security finally appealed with us to leave, and we did. Hector cranked up his bike and headed back to California.

Billie and the Boys

As I started out the gate, I spotted a discarded program slightly indented where someone had stepped on it while it was lying next to the walkway. I picked up the program, glanced at it and thought about tossing it away again. Then, I rolled it up and took it to the car. I still have the program.

The next morning when I awoke, the morning was crisp and the bedroom filled with the odor of fresh pine. It seemed a nice Flagstaff Sunday morning right up until the time I tried to move. My neck and shoulders were so painfully sore I literally could not lift them from the pillow.

I recalled a trainer coming through with a large brown bottle, passing out four aspirins to all takers and saying, "Take four more before you go to bed." I was so full of myself when I found the bed that I wasn't thinking about aspirin. I am uncertain that four aspirins before bed would have made any difference, but it couldn't have hurt.

Billie shook her head. She brought me four aspirins and a glass of water. Then, she told me to get up and come eat. I did, but it had to be a wretched sight that made its way to the kitchen table.

I ate left-handed. It would be noon before I could raise my right arm. Billie provided me with exactly the amount of sympathy she deemed I deserved.

It seems there were telephone calls exchanged between the wives. The collective stupidity of their husbands was the fundamental theme. Only the story of the plight of one fellow participant whose wife elected on this day to cook and straighten up the house in her most revealing garments during a time he could not lift his painful throbbing body from the couch brought good humor to my afternoon.

Coach Spilsbury called Monday evening to thank me and invite me to lunch. At lunch, he said that with pending conference changes, he could squeeze me out a year of eligibility. I considered it and declined. We could not move back to Cottage City.

Still, my relationship with Coach Spilsbury tightened. I was gaining a passion for teaching the game. For the first time since my odd disconnect had occurred around the time of my grandfather's grass fire, my interest in football was reignited. .

With all that said, I felt H&H was prospering, Flagstaff was growing, and I loved working with my brother.

CHAPTER TWENTY-TWO

Time to Go

A partnership insurance policy allowed Arnold to purchase Ralph's half of the business, but it did not provide money for inventory. Although the Christmas season had been brisk and the month over month business was increasing at an unexpected pace, the spring of 1961 found Arnold scrambling for money to purchase the required inventory.

In this era of restricted banking, the only banks in Flagstaff were two banks which operated statewide, First National Bank of Arizona, Valley National Bank, and one locally owned bank. By reputation, all three were conservative in their lending practices. There was little available money.

James and I were unaware of the depth of Arnold's cash flow difficulty. He did offer to sell me twenty-five percent of the business if I could borrow the money.

I discussed it with Billie. I believe we both liked the idea. Not knowing of Arnold's earlier efforts, I made the rounds of the banks. My efforts were unsuccessful, but I did really try. I suspect our Naugahyde furniture, now paid for, was less than impressive collateral.

Arnold then told us he had secured the money from a Phoenix bank and that his expectations for the business were so great that he was giving his wife's brother-in-law, Bob Artlip, a job.

Bob showed up, but he rarely worked. The summer was better than any of us had anticipated, but there was little help forthcoming from Bob. He spent his time in the office talking to Arnold and flirting with the bookkeeper. It seemed no flirtation was serious to Bob, but rather it was just a form of harmless social interaction.

In the beginning, James and I would just look at each other and shake our heads. We knew that if sales orders were to be taken and deliveries made, it would be our responsibility. So, we did our jobs and did them well. H & H was flourishing.

By early July, it was thriving beyond even Arnold's dreams. It was also prospering to the point that James and I really needed the help to keep the orders processing at the speed our customers expected from a local operation. Bob was becoming a nuisance and an annoyance.

A confrontation occurred on a Wednesday after James and I both had left around 6 AM on our appointed rounds. I returned after closing time to find that an order of one hundred pound sacks of flour for Jerry's Spudnut had not been delivered. Now getting 15 to 20 sacks of flour into the doughnut shop was our most difficult delivery. Despite its popularity, The Spudnut was still a small business. I knew Jerry didn't order flour until he needed flour.

Bob had stacked the flour on a pallet, sat it by the back door, and left for the day. I was tempted to just ignore the note for James or me, whoever got in first, to make the delivery, but I knew James would not ignore the note. Further, I knew Jerry likely needed the flour for the morning. I took off my good shirt, tossed it the pickup cab, loaded the flour, and delivered it.

I arrived home close to seven.

I have always been slow to anger, but enough was enough. The next morning, Arnold and I had a very direct conversation. It was a most unsatisfying exchange with a disappointing result. Arnold reluctantly acknowledged he had chosen not to disclose the full nature of Bob's employment. It wasn't an employment at all.

Bob had married the older sister of Arnold's wife. This sister had acquired what Arnold considered to be a substantial amount of money when her previous marriage ended either in death or divorce, I don't recall which. Viewing a partnership in H & H Wholesale as providing a reasonable amount of status in the community, she purchased half-interest in the company.

So Bob wasn't an employee; his wife was now the owner of Ralph Herbert's share in the business.

I was frustrated. I told Arnold, "Being a partner doesn't make him any the less lazy."

Arnold knew he was lazy but felt he could do little about it.

James was waiting in the warehouse. While he was none too pleased either, he was more accepting of the circumstances.

Billie and I now had several detailed discussions during the coming weeks. The thought of returning to Oklahoma had been lying just under the surface for a time, never really given voice until now. It became an open part of our dialogue.

There was much I liked about Flagstaff. Over the next weeks there were two offers we seriously considered but ultimately decided against. Sad to say, one of them involved a light beer distributorship, but I was convinced no one would ever be so silly as to buy weak beer. Well, so much for my marketing acumen.

I gave Arnold notice for August 15th and Billie, already on leave from Mountain States, told them of her intentions.

Within days, Arnold came to me offering a large increase in salary. I asked why Bob was not with him. He said Bob wasn't fully on board with it yet, but would be. I declined.

I am unsure of the discussions James and Wilma might have had. I do know that of all of us, Wilma liked Flagstaff the most.

Wilma's feelings were somewhat the opposite of Billie's. Billie missed her sisters. Wilma wanted to keep James as far away from my parents as she could.

Now and again I have wondered if my brother's life would have been different had we remained in Flagstaff.

That is a game of "what if" that I cannot productively play.

The last task James and I performed together in Arizona was to load our U-Haul trailer. The refrigerator was placed in the front of the trailer and we then packed the shelves with our towels, linens, and clothing. We thoughtfully loaded and filled every conceivable space. We would load and check the tires of the trailer as if either of us actually understood how trailer tires would respond to the weight of our load.

With a box spring tied over the right wheel well, we hit the road, reverse Okies headed home.

And that was that.

Not lost
Just don't know
Where he's going
But his beard
Keeps on growing
Burma Shave

CHAPTER TWENTY-THREE

Took Us Back to Tulsa

This fall day at the Tulsa State Fair was warmer than most. We had made a full day of it, and the boys were thoroughly exhausted. We were making our way out toward the exit that would take us into the southeast parking lot, a space now occupied by a water park. I was carrying Mike, now two and a half, on my shoulders. Billie had David by the hand and he was walking beside us.

We were so deep in conservation that we barely noticed the little girl running beside us, trying to get our attention. Then, this strong male voice shouted from behind us, "Billie Jean!" Billie recognized the familiar tenor voice and stopped in her tracks. She turned and looked behind us. Jay Reynolds' voice had penetrated the clamor of a state fair crowd.

There in the crowd behind us was Billie's sister, Annice, and her husband with their three children, Freddie, Karen Sue, and Barbara Ann. They were making their way toward the exit when Annice spotted us in the midst of this flowing throng of tired people. After the hugs and handshakes and the exchanges of "what are you doing here" had taken place, we moved against a fence, out of the flow. We began to exchange explanations as to why we were in Tulsa and at the Tulsa State Fair.

They knew we had moved back to Oklahoma, but they believed we were living in Oklahoma City. We thought they were in Bartlesville. We had been in Tulsa just over a week. The telephone company was promoting Jay and transferring him to a location in Tulsa. Jay was already at his new job while Annice was still in Bartlesville making the arrangements to move the family.

Billie was ecstatic at the thought of having Annice and her family so near. I felt real affirmation that we had made the correct move for us.

From our earliest discussions of returning to Oklahoma, Tulsa was our preference. We both liked Tulsa. But we were repeatedly told the job market and the cost of living was more favorable in Oklahoma City. In the larger scheme of things, a solid job was priority one.

Leaving our loaded U-Haul in Norman with Ray Tucker, we made a hurried trip to Stigler and Sallisaw. We returned to Oklahoma City and rented a really nice duplex. We unloaded our furniture and got the trailer returned hours before the deadline. By the time I got back, Billie had the living room arranged and was lining the kitchen cabinets with shelf paper that she had brought from Stigler.

Accustomed to Flagstaff prices, everything in Oklahoma seemed so inexpensive. However, it was not so inexpensive that I didn't immediately begin the search for employment.

Using a recommended agency, I quickly got interviews with two companies. I was optimistic but anxious.

My first interview was with Bill Bowers of Liberty Mutual Insurance Company, a smallish man filled with non-productive over-activity. He was enthused about his new position as District Sales Manager. I left the office feeling the interview had gone well.

I had an interview scheduled with Pitney-Bowes for the next morning. Using a pay phone at a service station, I checked with the agency and found I had a message to call Mr. Bowers. I went for a second interview involving several people. I was hired in the property and casualty sales division on the condition I would relocate to Tulsa. Now someone has to be looking out for you to catch that kind of break.

Once hired, Liberty Mutual paid the agency fee. After a six week training period in Oklahoma City, all of the expenses involved in our relocation to Tulsa would be paid. I couldn't wait to get home and tell Billie.

Billie seemed to be pleased. There is something affirming about employment.

For the six weeks of training, we lived in a duplex in Oklahoma City.

Billie and the Boys

Although our stay in the City was brief, we connected with my cousin, Linda Jane. She and her husband, Stanley Skaer, who was a medical student at the University of Oklahoma, were living in the same set of duplexes. With being back in Oklahoma a contributing factor, Billie seemed to find something restorative in her relationship with Linda Jane.

Relocated in Tulsa, we finally settled into a nice rental house on East Latimer just to the east of Memorial and a short two block walk to John Ross Elementary School. David attended Kindergarten at Ross.

During this period, I had a brief reunion with a close boyhood friend, a friend born the day before me, Jimmy Thomas. He was now out of the military, married to his wife, Gerri, and they were living in Tulsa. While the overlap was brief, the part I most recall was so typically Jimmy. He and Gerri came to our home to listen to the OU-Syracuse football game, the game of Joe Don Looney's sprint into Sooner football lore. He was virtually jumping on the couch with excitement.

We had a few lunches before life took Jimmy toward Oklahoma City. Not so many years ago, through Jimmy's efforts, I got a birthday telephone call from him. We only got together one more time at a gathering in Stigler in August of 2009, but we never lost contact again.

I wouldn't see Gerri again until June 17, 2010 when, along with his family and a few of our Stigler friends, we gathered under what shade could be found in the Stigler Cemetery to bury Jimmy's ashes between his parent's graves.

Bobby Cariker said the right words, graciously thanking Jim's adult family for returning him to his boyhood home. Bobby's wife, Nancy Gail (Cumpton), Noretta (Parsons) Livesay, and Sue Nell Gulley sang. All were friends from our childhoods.

Downtown Tulsa of 1962 was a pleasant and stimulating place. It brimmed with activity. The sidewalks were full of men in basic blue or black suits and white shirts, ties only slightly more colorful than the suits, formal but required. Women wore dresses, substantially more colorful but no less proper. The constant ebb and flow of this stream was redirected only by the irregular islands created by window shoppers.

Window shopping, while a condensed version can still be observed in large malls, is virtually a lost art form. One must now go to Utica Square to behold genuine visual evidence of a residual form of this social intercourse. Window shopping requires a couple to communicate their dreams in a rather tangible format. Both understood that what was being communicated was a hope, a wish, and not an immediate expectation. If they truly value it, the discriminating couple can still find the experience.

The building in which in which I worked, an office space I thought to be so nice, no longer stands. The Franklin Building was located on the northeast corner of 4th Street and Boulder Avenue, a space now occupied by a Tulsa World parking lot with a bronze statue of a paper boy on a bicycle, also a small monument to an era now past, standing on the corner.

Those of us whose jobs required us to come in and out of the office were provided with valet parking at the Mayo Parking Garage on Cheyenne adjacent to the downtown Sears and Roebuck's store.

While one day each week was put aside for the business man's plate at Danner's Cafeteria within Utica Square, there was also sitting at school desks and eating hot dogs or three-ways at the Coney place only a half-block away and burgers at the dining room in the Downtowner Motel. There were juicy, red-in-the-middle burgers with clients and friends at Goldie's Patio Grill located in the pro shop of the par 3 Golf Course on the southwest corner of 51st and Lewis.

A frequent lunch or post-lunch hangout became the pool hall beneath the Tulsa World building. Only a small neon billiards sign announced its existence to the general public. You walked under the sign and down a rather narrow stairway of well-worn concrete steps bounded by aging iron rails that were hand polished to a gleaming grey. There were snooker tables to the front and pool tables to the rear with a centerpiece of one actual billiard table. The felt was well kept and the slate rolled true, and there was the occasional burn in the wood where a light cigarette had been allowed to lay too long simply added to the ambience of the hall.

Lunch consisted of pre-packaged sandwiches carrying the questionable guarantee of "made fresh daily" on the wrapper, a Coca-Cola, and a game of snooker.

Above this splendid billiard hall, you could stand on the sidewalk and watch the huge press, with its seemly endless rolls of spinning paper, print the next issue of the Tulsa World or the Tulsa Tribune, depending upon the time of day. Having been fascinated with simply drinking a coke and watching Dad Bankhead print the Haskell County Tribune on a clearly dated press, I was always impressed. If the press was running, I always paused to gaze though the window with some degree of wonder. Other times, when the press was idle, I would just stop for a moment, hoping it might start. I suppose because I personally have such limited mechanical skills, I have always been intrigued by such machines.

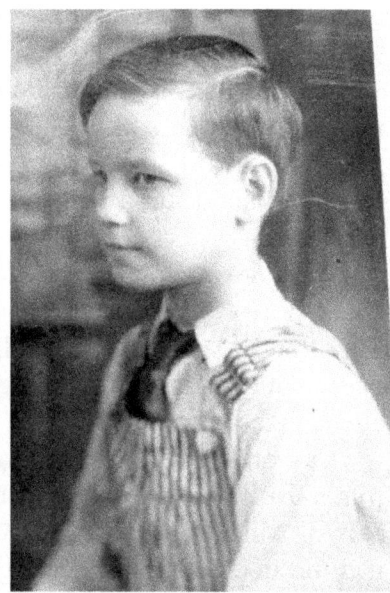

CHAPTER TWENTY-FOUR

Jay Boy

Annice and Jay were now comfortably residing on 21st Street near Memorial Avenue. They carefully selected this house for its proximity to an excellent Tulsa Public School complex that combined McArthur Elementary School, Whitney Junior High School, and culminated with Nathan Hale High School. Such were the Tulsa Public Schools in the 1960's.

My brother-in-law was a man of many passions. Given a challenge, his enthusiasm could become boundless.

We played regular games of ten point pitch. Annice, Billie, and I enjoyed the games, but Jay was zealous about them. Billie was always his partner. Even if there no other options when a losing card was laid upon the table, Jay would bellow.

One evening as a very competitive game was moving toward a conclusion, with one card left to play, Billie examined her card, calmly reached behind her and closed the window. Then, while staring at Jay, she laid the losing card on the table. Upon cue, Jay

Billie and the Boys

roared his displeasure until the laughter moved around the table to him.

His use of the language could be colorful with definitions unique to him, or so it seemed. Mucket could be an adjective or a noun. He swore that everyone in Sequoyah County knew the word and understood its meaning. So, no further explanation was necessary.

The downtown Tulsa Christmas Parade was an event that could not be missed. The bands were large, colorful and loud. The floats were always well made, filled with the pride of participation. Despite seemingly always bitter cold weather, our attendance was compulsory.

Jay and I went early to secure an ideal place on the parade route. Billie and Annice would come later with the children. David, Mike, Barbara, and Susie, tightly wrapped in blankets, had the finest curbside seating Jay could arrange. Freddie would try to stand until the cold would send him to the curb and under the blankets.

Every available thermos was filled with hot chocolate or coffee. Jay provided the family with a running commentary of the parade. No child was happier to see the arrival of Santa's sleigh than Jay.

Understand that Jay did not play favorites. He loved every holiday.

One Halloween, Jay outdid himself. His costume was a granny dress, and the gimmick was comprised of large red Christmas tree lights and a mercury switch. He wired the costume so that when he raised his arms, his wig, hands, and chest lit up. The child who would stand their ground from the glowing breast and the clutching, grasping arms of the cackling witch was well rewarded.

Word rapidly spread of the glowing crazy woman and the reward of a full size candy bar for the courageous. Kids flocked to the Reynolds' front door, many bringing their unsuspecting friends for a Halloween jolt.

In an era when all significant bowl games were played on New Year's Day, we brought our television set to Annice and

Jay's family room to be stacked on top of their set so that two games could be watched at once. It was a full day of family fun, food, and football.

As to football, Jay and I attended many high school games over the years. It was the state championship game of either 1962 or 1963 involving the Lindsey Leopards that is clearly the most memorable. However, it was not the game, but the circumstances that made this particular game memorable. At the time, only the district champions advanced to the playoffs, but the classifications were larger, so the playoffs still extended well into the cold weather season.

This championship game was scheduled for Skelly Stadium at the University of Tulsa. There was a highly recruited quarterback playing for Lindsey that Jay was excited about watching. By the Wednesday before the Saturday night game, he had everyone rowed up and ready to be in attendance.

On late Thursday afternoon, an Oklahoma winter storm laid a thin layer of ice on the ground which shortly became covered by several inches of snow. By Friday at noon, the snow lightened and passed as the temperatures plunged into the single digits and the northwest wind increased.

Following a morning of uncertainty, we found that despite the most inclement of conditions, the game was going to be played as scheduled. Billie and Annice quickly decided they would not attend. The more the ladies made of the weather, nasty even by northeastern Oklahoma standards, the more determined Jay became that he was going to see the young man play.

With the probability that the temperature would be in teens at kickoff and drop from there, Jay began to plot methods by which we might remain moderately warm. Beyond coats, blankets, and thermoses filled with black coffee, he decided upon a metal pail, charcoal, and lighter fluid.

With our portable heating device covered by layers of blankets, we bought our tickets. The ticket taker, certainly every inch as cold as we were, waved us through the gate. We went up the nearest east side ramp and positioned ourselves so that the walls of the ramp served to block the north wind while not obstructing our view.

Billie and the Boys

We fired up our heater and prepared for kickoff.

By the end of the first quarter, with several other fans now warming themselves over small fires of newspapers on the concrete floors of the stadium, we felt secure that the glowing coals in our heating bucket would not concern anyone. By halftime, we had attracted a genuine circle of friends.

We left very early in the fourth quarter, pleased to have been in attendance, leaving the heating pail and the remaining charcoal with our newly acquired friends.

If such things are possible, Jay came by his love of all things holiday through family transmission.

Every Christmas is important, each unique in its own manner, and over the years I have had the opportunity to participate in the Christmas rituals of a number of families. Jay's family produced the most consistently entertaining and agreeable Christmases I ever encountered.

The Reynolds family Christmas celebration began on Christmas Eve and was centered in the home of Jay's parents, Otto and Gazelle Reynolds. Ott, who I recall as a small, sinewy man, was a light-hearted, carefree individual who seemed to view work as a day to day thing. Gazelle, small and frail in appearance, was a serious woman who rarely, if ever, missed a day of work at Holder's Dry Goods. Holder's, the Hays and Buchanan of Sallisaw, was owned by her father, who I only knew as "Poncho."

Ott and Gazelle prized all four of their children. Of the two I knew well, their eldest daughter, Lelia Jean, was much her mother's child. Jay, the most honest and hard working man I ever knew, was an intriguing blend of both.

The home was a small shotgun house with the only bath contained in a dog-eared room attached to the kitchen, appearing to have been an architectural afterthought. The kitchen table hosted a boisterous Christmas poker game in which the players would come and go, a game that would persist without interruption until Santa's arrival on Christmas morning.

Thick cigarette smoke rose from the table until it inundated the entire the kitchen and the adjacent living room. I was never in any room anywhere that could outdo the density of smoke that hovered over that table.

Leila Jean supervised the creation of the refreshment center piece which was affectionately referred to as "The Bucket." The recipe for this concoction included a fifth of bourbon and a fifth of vodka. As the vestiges of prohibition lingered and bootleggers thrived in eastern Oklahoma, the brand depended often upon availability.

A large metal bucket for a lid was required. In a pinch, any bucket would do. In fact, on one particularly harsh and blustery Christmas Eve, it was discovered that no one had secured the required bucket. Ott surveyed the situation, went to a shed out behind the house, and retrieved his minnow bucket. After a reasonably intense cleansing, the "Bucket" was made in Ott's shiner bucket, so I've been told.

Once an acceptable bucket is secured, it is half-filled with ice. Several cans of frozen concentrated orange juice direct from the container and a half a can of any other frozen citrus concentrate other than grapefruit was placed into the ice and alcohol. Then, the lid was sealed on the bucket.

It was then stirred by rotating the bucket with a twisting wrist moving the bucket in a circular motion until a heavy coat of frost formed on the outside of the bucket.

By every Sallisaw accounting, Leila Jean's bucket had a substantial local following. Any number of people would stop by to express their Christmas wishes and partake in the good cheer. This blend of Christmas spirit and the spirits of the bucket gave rise to many adventures and misadventures.

Leila Jean was married to Ray Farmer, who with his brother Cherry, owned the Sallisaw Western Auto Store. Christmas required the delivery of a number of bicycles that been carefully assembled in the rear of the store during the weeks preceding Christmas Eve. The back of the Western Auto during the bicycle assembly time was a favorite seasonal haunt of many Sallisaw businessmen. The Farmer brothers took great pride in their Christmas bicycles.

Billie and I had the genuine privilege of buying such a bicycle for each of our sons during the time we lived in Sallisaw.

Billie and the Boys

Regardless, delivery of the bikes late on Christmas Eve was the tour de force. While the whole concept of placing a new bike on the porch of a child with the belief that it would still be there when the child awoke on Christmas morning might be unrealistic in this day and age, but it worked in the 1950's and 1960's.

The bikes were loaded in the bed of a pickup which was then driven to within a block of the assigned home. Then it would be ridden to the home and carefully placed in a predetermined position, most often on the front or back porch.

Very often, the bicycle riding Santa would be well fortified against the December chill by the contents of the "Bucket." However, I do not believe any toys were ever more lovingly and joyously dispensed than those delivered by these bucket-fueled Santa Clauses.

This Christmas Eve gathering gave rise to many other legends such as the evening a mattress was placed on the floor for the youngest family members to sleep, inadvertently trapping the cat. The cat was not missed until morning and was discovered only when the mattress was removed to allow space for the opening of gifts. The cat wobbled out and is said to have still been wobbling a number of days later.

While I cannot attest to this latter story, it is well ingrained in Reynolds family lore.

CHAPTER TWENTY-FIVE

Oiler Baseball

In the spring of 1962, Billie and Annice had left for Sallisaw with the kids to get an early start on the Memorial Day weekend. Jay and I were driving down after work the next day.

With a night to pass, Jay suggested a Tulsa Oilers baseball game.

The stadium had a central entrance. Greeting you, painted in the center of a dark blue backdrop, was a large baseball with feet and a capped head on which the team name, "Oilers," was prominently displayed. Beneath it all was the proud proclamation of an affiliation with the St. Louis Cardinals. Either by the name of Oiler Stadium or Texas League Field, this was a classic baseball park. While to some the well painted large wooden structure may have appeared less than impressive, I considered it inspiring. I had seen a number of games at Athletic Stadium, home of the Muskogee entry in the Class C Western Association, so I had high expectations. Just walking up to the ball park clearly far exceeded my expectations.

As we stood in line to purchase our tickets, the chatter around us was of baseball. "How'd the Cardinals do today?" "Da ya know who's throwin' tonight?" "Hear the lefty that was so tough on us last year is still with this bunch."

Carrying their wares, vendors called to you, "Hot dogs, peanuts, crackerjacks," "Ice cold beer," and "Coca-Cola." Draught beer at the concession was cheaper but not colder.

It smelled and sounded like baseball.

While the lighting beneath the stands was dim, it was adequate to assist you in making your way to an entrance ramp. You could hear the rumble of stomping feet above you as you moved toward the ramp. You walked up the incline and emerged

Billie and the Boys

through the opening. With a final single stride, you stepped out of the dim and into the bright lights.

There it was. A baseball field of deep, dark green well manicured grass into which an infield had been meticulously cut and then smoothed by rake and drag. The outfield walls were covered with advertising. U-Need-Um Tires to OTSCO to the D-X Sunray scoreboard on which balls, strikes, outs, a hit, or an error were displayed by lights. The score by inning was still proudly hung by hand.

When you stepped from beneath the cover of a ramp, there was a detonation of sensory excitement. It was without mistake a baseball field. It was exciting.

At pivotal moments, a strong voice would rise from somewhere behind home plate, "L-E-T-S GOOOOOOO TULSA!"

It was way better than Athletic Park in Muskogee. It was Tulsa Oiler baseball.

I could not wait to bring Billie and the boys to see it.

And for years to come, see it we did. Often taking advantage of a promotional night of some variety or another and always purchasing general admission, we felt we had squatter's rights in those red bench seats about level with the first base bag.

CHAPTER TWENTY-SIX

A Home of Our Own

In the Spring of 1963, we bought our first home, a house at 628 South 105th Place East. Billie and Annice had been in search of a house for several months when Billie found the perfect house. It was located on a cul-de-sac where two other families with Sallisaw roots were living. Betty and Dale Furlow were directly across the street, and Tommy Westmoreland and his wife lived at the north end of the circle.

It was a traditional home for the time, with three bedrooms, one bath, and a very nice kitchen with a bronze colored built-in stove and oven and even a garbage disposal. It was new construction with hardwood floors throughout except in the kitchen and the bath. However, the decisive sales point was a huge old ash tree in the front yard. All this opulence came with a price of only $12,750.00.

After an excruciatingly close examination of the state of our personal finances, Billie and I decided we could afford it. Now if we could just convince FHA.

I felt it to be a truly splendid house. We were ecstatic with the idea of homeownership.

Now, for the first and only time, we experienced the horror of the FHA loan closing process. In the downtown offices of Mercury Mortgage Company, Billie and I sat across the desk from an older gentleman. We made every effort to appear as mature and responsible as possible, listening to his flinty sermon on financial responsibility and homeownership while pointing out the great personal commitment a twenty-five year home loan represented. It felt a bit like we were agreeing to make payments until the Rapture.

Billie and the Boys

After a number of "Yes, sir" or "No, sir" responses, we signed our names on a seemingly endless number of dotted lines.

All done, he smiled, gave us the house keys and congratulated us on our new status in the community as tax paying homeowners. As we exited the elevator and walked toward the door, we both acknowledged that there were segments of the experience we found to be very disquieting. I believe we said something like, "Wow!" We were euphoric to have actually bought a home.

Backyard baseball now had a home field. Weather permitting, back yard games of catch and fielding ground balls had become the favored pastime on many summer evenings. In their father's mind, the talent of our boys was unquestionably in the superior range.

It seems every southern poet or songwriter has composed some ode to the joy of summer evenings. If I had that talent, I would compose an affirmation to Oklahoma summer evenings and backyard baseball with the boys.

Somewhere in here, Billie's enthusiasm for modernistic white Naugahyde furniture diminished. Early American, particularly the Ethan Allen brand carried by Rich's Furniture located on Peoria Avenue, became the furniture fashion of choice. Soon pieces of Ethan Allen living room furniture from Rich's and a maple kitchen table with chairs secured from Eads Brothers in Fort Smith were in our home. We were very proud of our new house.

Billie moved the white Naugahyde couch with the matching white coffee table and end table into the empty bedroom, the bedroom nearest the kitchen, converting it into a television room. It was large enough to be functional and small enough to be intimate. Truth be told, as a family, this became an exceedingly agreeable room.

I would hear of the ritual afternoon viewings of a local children's program, "Tuffy and Mr. Zing". On Mike's fifth birthday, Billie and Annice made the necessary arrangements to take the kids to Channel 8 for the show.

As Mr. Zing acknowledged Mike, Mike reached into the pocket of his new green and black plaid sport coat as if to retrieve something he had brought to give to Mr. Zing.

Mr. Zing said, "I see you have brought me something."

Mike handed him the slip of paper he had taken from his pocket.

Then to the live television audience Mr. Zing read, "Inspected by number four."

Mike smiled admiringly at the momentarily puzzled Mr. Zing.

In some corner of the room Billie's face was flushing Irish red.

We watched so many television programs together, the four of us. We watched The Jetsons, The Beaver, and the Beverly Hillbillies. Rawhide was rapidly becoming a favorite.

As it was with my grandfather, Red Skelton was compulsory viewing and the one program the boys were allowed to remain up a bit later to watch. However, on many evenings by its conclusion, Mike would be asleep on the couch with his head in my lap and his feet on Billie's leg.

Local news was Channel 8. Jack Morris reported the news, Don Woods with Gusty was a reliable forecaster of the weather and he seemed to so enjoy his work, and Hal O'Halloran brought us the sports. Their 15 minute newscast concluded our evening.

The boys tucked into their beds, Billie and I would sit on the couch watching television and talking. I still consider these times to be among the sweetest of life's confections.

Even though they are now deep into adulthood, Billie is still on occasion asked about the differences in our boys. She always says that she could sit David in the yard and tell him not to leave an area. She could come back and find David exactly in the prescribed spot. If told to walk a certain path home from school, he walked that path. Mike, on the other hand, was known to be chased home by coyotes. The mail carrier would bring him home because he would follow him on his route around the cul-de-sac and talk to him ceaselessly. Mike never met a delivery man he didn't like.

Billie and the Boys

On the corner of the lot to the south of us was a sizeable red ant hill. Our first summer in our home, Mike's curiosity about the banned ant hill was boundless. Mike would come yelling and hopping across the lawn, his hands slapping and thrashing, trying to remove his red ant infested shorts and tee shirt.

Behavioral science would predict that the negative consequences of one or two such experiences would be adequate to extinguish his inquisitiveness. Such a hypothesis, adamantly endorsed by behavioral scientists such as myself, proved to be invalid. Convinced that Mike's exploratory interest in the social complexity of red ant society would not soon fade, we destroyed the ant hill.

Then again, maybe he just liked stomping on ants.

I do not know why such times do not last. I only know they don't.

We took a road trip to Flagstaff. Following a dandy lunch at the Shamrock Dairy Queen, we stayed the night at the Travelodge at Tucumcari. Quite unexpectedly, we discovered that the cast from the television program <u>Rawhide</u> was also staying at the Travelodge while filming outdoor segments for the show. It made for an exciting evening of looking for recognizable faces at the pool or on the walkways. Had we known life's complete plot, we would have paid much closer attention to a young Clint Eastwood rather than to Eric Fleming who portrayed the trail boss, Gil Favor.

Regardless, as we pulled out onto Route 66 the next morning, I am certain someone in the car said, "Head'em up! Move'em Out!" We took to the open road with Frankie Lane's theme song playing in our heads.

We stayed with Connie and Lamar. The campus was changing, and Cottage City had been leveled to make way for new construction. Oak Creek, Flagstaff Country Club, the El Charro, and Miz Zip were visited.

We spent four days on the road and four days in Flagstaff, taking photographs of the boys on the lava flows near Grants. This was a pleasant trip that is memorable for a chance encounter in Tucumcari. I have discovered with road trips over the years that the nicest part is arriving in front of our home.

CHAPTER TWENTY-SEVEN

November 22, 1963

Even in recollection, it seems it was just a November Friday morning. The weather was decidedly undecided. We were paying close attention to the weather forecast with Thanksgiving now only six days away and looking forward to the weekend. It seems we were expecting the weather to turn much colder, but it hadn't yet.

I'm certain Don Woods, the first real television meteorologist in Tulsa, was the source of our expectation. His drawings of Gusty would then visually imprint his weather forecast. I know it was before distinct county lines began to appear on weather maps and Dad observed, "You can always find Haskell County. It looks like a Scotty dog." He was right.

I only wore my suit coat. You remember such things because there are days whose events tend to make you forgetful.

At lunch I had hung my suit coat on a hanger against the west wall of the pool hall below the Tulsa World building. I was eating lunch and deeply engrossed in a game of snooker when the first whispers begin to make their way from table to table, radiating from those closest to the radio behind the counter along the west wall.

At first, there were just whispers about shots being fired at the Presidential motorcade in Dallas, and the chatter of the balls quieted some but not a lot. Then, the man behind the counter relayed that President Kennedy might have been wounded and the pool hall drew silent as many begin to strain to hear the small radio behind the counter.

A couple of us from Liberty Mutual left and returned to the office. I called Billie. She said that she had been waxing the hardwood floor in the boy's bedroom. She had stopped for a bite of lunch and to watch "As the World Turns" when a bulletin

Billie and the Boys

concerning the President and his motorcade in Dallas interrupted programming. I told Billie I was coming home.

I made a quick stop to retrieve the suit coat that, in my preoccupation, I had left hanging in the pool hall. The place seemed to be empty, strangely silent.

The boys were not yet home from school. Billie and I sat fixed in front of the television. We heard that the President had been taken to Parkland Memorial Hospital. There were moments of hope.

I don't know if we actually watched it the first time or if we have just seen it so often over the years, but we both believe we looked on as Walter Cronkite removed his glasses, looked up at a clock on the wall, and told us President Kennedy had died.

Over the following days on black and white television, we learned of Lee Harvey Oswald and then Jack Ruby; we heard of Dealey Plaza and the Texas School Book Depository and wondered about the contents of something called the Zapruder film.

In the long intervals between news presentations, a string quartet performed somber pieces.

Somewhere in the midst of it all, after much discussion and to the consternation of many, Oklahoma and Nebraska played a football game. The Sooners lost.

Conspiracy theories expanded and contracted and expanded again. Responsibility was assigned to Cuba and Fidel Castro or to organized crime. I found it disquieting that such an event could be the result of the atypical notions of a single man. During a conversation about a month later, Dad said something close to, "People believe they know, but they don't and might never."

On television, we watched as our Nation said its goodbyes to the young President who had seemed to represent all the optimism and vitality of post-war America.

The news anchor I deemed most credible, Walter Cronkite, seemed to be overwhelmed at times by the events, adding to his humanity and credibility with me. I always believed he somehow really did "get it."

The assassinations of Robert Kennedy and Martin Luther King would follow. My willingness to believe that the actions a single individual in a flawed delusional state could profoundly alter the very nature of our national discourse grew.

We waged war upon poverty and lost. Civil rights were secured for many, but we never understood that the true social disparity in our world was financial. It is wealth that separates us.

We sent young men to fight a war in Vietnam where it seemed our goal was impasse and even that seemed subject to repetitive redefinition. To our national shame, our returning veterans were treated dishonorably. We sent them there, many simply because they did not have the means to avoid being drafted. They served and honored us far better than we merited. Still too often, it is not their personal sacrifices, not their efforts nor their heroic deeds that are recalled. It is the shamefulness of conduct of a very tiny few.

Our sense of national identity seemed profoundly altered. We became increasingly unsure of who we were as a Nation and as a people. We came to focus upon our flaws and frailties as if our strengths as a country and as a people had simply vanished, becoming legends of a storied past.

Our trust impaired, we looked for deception, and we found it.

I feel complicit.

CHAPTER TWENTY-EIGHT

Silver Bells

James left H&H Wholesale and Flagstaff. After an extremely brief return to Oklahoma, James and his family retraced their steps and located in Winslow, Arizona. He secured his first job in law enforcement with the City of Winslow. My brother was a policeman.

Our contact became limited, but they seemed happy in Winslow. I never knew why they returned to Oklahoma but they did. James took a position on the Norman Police Department.

This is a time in my brother's life that still has a considerable vagueness for me. I know certain truths and believe other things to be true.

James enjoyed being a member of the Norman Police Department. I believe he was a fine officer. I believe that here my brother found a sense of purpose that made him proud of who he was. It is so complicated to find and so effortlessly lost.

We made trips to Norman to visit and to watch Oklahoma football games. My brother took great pride in his role in directing the crowd flow in and out of such events. Still, mostly we visited in Stigler.

James was clearly a hail fellow well met. He seemed to fit easily into the Norman community.

He was developing a passion for buying and trading coins. While I was accumulating Mercury head dimes and Walking Liberty half-dollars only to ultimately lose them to a car thief, James was beginning to collect gold coins. He was proud of his coins and would excitedly call about a new acquisition.

Through his coin trading and his police work, he became a close friend of Earl Simpson. Earl had Sallisaw roots and operated several pawn shops in the Norman area. Earl introduced James to diamonds and other stones. Through Earl, he made the acquaintance of a young Norman jeweler with a very wide creative bent.

Feeling that we were doing well financially, I arrived at the Christmas I wanted a special gift for Billie's Christmas. As it is with gifts, I was in my customary clueless state.

During a Stigler visit, James suggested I consider having a piece of jewelry made. He suggested the stones could be obtained from Earl at an affordable price and his friend would make the piece. I gave him an idea as to the amount of money I felt I could spend. He said he'd call me.

Up in the week, James called from the jeweler's establishment. We visited for a bit before a female voice in background told him to ask me what came to mind when I thought of my wife and Christmas. Many commonplace questions might have stumped me cold. This one I knew.

"Silver Bells."

He expressed his bewilderment. I explained I was thinking of the Christmas song, Silver Bells. It was clearly her favorite and had been since I had known her.

When she was sixteen and out of school for the Christmas recess, Billie went to Fort Smith to visit her sister, Pauline. Pauline was a R.N., freshly minted by St. Edward's School of Nursing and now employed by the hospital. She was living in a small apartment near her work. At the time, St. Edward's Hospital was located just out of downtown Fort Smith toward the upper end of Garrison Avenue.

Billie was walking back toward the apartment from a day of Christmas shopping in downtown Fort Smith. Dusk was approaching when she heard the bells from Immaculate Conception Church start to chime, seeming to blend with the Christmas music echoing from a department store. As the song and the bells seemed to merge into a perfect harmony, it began to snow. The song was Silver Bells.

She never forgot the sounds or the sight, nor the feelings of Christmas they stirred in her. It always kindles the sensation that all is as it should be and everything is in its place.

At times, she has spontaneously retold me story as if somehow I had never hear it. If you ever heard her tell it, you could never forget it. It is a beautiful story and there is peace in its telling.

I explained the significance of Silver Bells. He first suggested a necklace of silver bells with small diamonds set as the clappers. It just didn't sound right. He said to give him some time to think about other possibilities.

James called me within the week and said, "Silver leaves."

He described a ring with diamonds and sapphires, her birth stone, in a setting of silver leaves. It was a creative idea and it pleased me. A deal was struck. A ring was created.

We followed our usual Christmas Eve route. First, a lovely rather formal dinner at Lou and Charles' home with a meal prepared by Frances Medeiros, likely with aid of her sister, Geraldine. All of Billie's sisters and their families were there. As always, names for Christmas gifts had been drawn during Thanksgiving. If you weren't present, someone drew for you. The family joke was if you didn't show up, you got the names of our Christmas hosts. I don't think anyone enjoyed the joke more than Charles.

We stopped at Ott and Gazelle's home. As the driver, I would only take the requisite sip from the bucket before becoming completely immersed in this warm, embracing holiday milieu. The room rang with laughter and good natured but direct ribbings.

Then, it was a midnight sleigh ride over Wild Horse Mountain to Stigler. We quietly slipped in the back door so as not to awaken Shari and Sandy in the mistaken belief that Santa Claus had arrived. James and Wilma often waited up for us.

Our entry was never so quiet that Mother wasn't promptly in the back room with us to assure herself everyone had made the Sallisaw sleigh ride safely. She would have the hide-a-way bed from the couch ready. The cushions would be converted into beds for the boys.

This Christmas, James didn't greet us at the door. Wilma and Mother were telling everyone that he had forgotten some gifts and had returned to Norman for them.

Then, in a quiet moment, Wilma whispered, "He forgot Billie's gift." He didn't realize the gift hadn't traveled with them until he went to secure it for Mother to see before it was wrapped.

So, after having completed the two and a half hour trip only an hour or so earlier, my brother departed on Christmas Eve to retrace his route to Norman and retrieve Billie's Christmas gift.

During the very wee hours of that Christmas morning, I received a gift from my brother far greater than any for which I would have ever ask. He drove the distance from Norman to Stigler three times that night for no reason other than to allow me to give my wife a special gift on Christmas morning.

James awakened me when he arrived. The small stones superbly displayed made the ring seem even grander that I had hoped. My brother, now in his sleeveless undershirt, and me in whatever passed for pajamas, sat on the living room floor with an ottoman between us and wrapped Billie's ring by the lights of the Christmas tree. Then, we placed it deep in the stack of presents near the base of the tree.

Billie got a ring that I received as a special delivery gift from my brother.

To this day, I don't know how we kept it secret from Billie. Billie, the youngest little Martin girl, who was known to slyly remove the tape from a package for a peek, didn't find out. But we did.

I think.

CHAPTER TWENTY-NINE

The Boys and Baseball

David discovered from his friend next door, Larry Woodson, that there was a second grade baseball team allowing first graders to try out. He came home and asked if he could try out. His mother told him to talk to me. I told him to find out when and where, and I would take him. I really thought that would be the end of it.

But David greeted me the next afternoon, glove in hand, and said that the tryout was in the field to the south of the school building. So, I took him.

Elgin Harris whose son, Vic, was also a first grader was organizing a team, the East Central Steelers. My sons were very fortunate. Elgin was the finest baseball coach that I have ever encountered at any level. He had a great passion for the game and the knack for teaching it to boys.

Elgin took an interest in David. Although physically small, David could throw the ball with an unexpected velocity and surprising accuracy. From hours and years of backyard baseball games, he could hit.

David hung onto Elgin's every instruction, seeming to absorb even the smallest detail. David and Vic became fast friends.

After about a week, Mike began to accompany us to David's practices. Then, Mike showed up with his glove and bat. Although too young to take part, he was appointed batboy. He took his duties very seriously.

Soon, daylight willing, Mike would be the last boy to take batting practice and to fly under Elgin's very large wing. Mike had fun and his skills grew.

With consistency and commitment, Elgin moved a team that before an early season game an opposing coach referred to as "leftovers and first graders" to winning the Northeast Tulsa Youth baseball association's season ending tournament.

Over the next four seasons, with Elgin's tutoring, David's skills increased and his knowledge of the game grew.

Billie developed an understanding of the game to go with her passion for all things her sons did. Today, I will state that her knowledge of football and basketball far exceeds the typical male who might consider himself an expert in such arenas. Let me be clearer in my statement: Billie knows basketball and football better than most who are actively coaching those sports at the high school level.

Over the years, she only drew one clear line: "I will not keep the scorebook." She won't diagram sentences, either.

We discovered that Elgin, his wife, Coleen, and Vic were also Tulsa Oiler fans with an affinity for first base seating. We watched baseball. David, Mike, and Vic were off with their friends, all over and under the stadium. They knew to be back by the bottom of the seventh inning, and they always were. Such were the times.

The East Central school district became a part of the Tulsa Public Schools and the East Central Steelers became the Reed Steelers.

After Reed Steelers games, we would go to Shakey's Pizza on Admiral. The boys stood on benches and looked through the windows as the pizza was prepared. We sat at long picnic style tables enjoying a pitcher of beer as pizza was prepared; sausage and black olive was preferred. Soon, other families began to join us. By season's end, the Reed Steelers had become a social group. It would stay so throughout our time with the Reed Steelers.

Kerr Elementary School would be opened and district lines were modified. The Steelers absorbed players from other squads. Billy Beard and Rodney Eckland left while Kevin Eidson and Mark Messick joined the squad. The families changed, but the dynamics of the team remained.

I got to coach a year of flag football. Kevin's ability to make difficult snaps allowed us to do many things. A quick and strong lineman, Bill Vining, gave Vic and David the edges with his solid and consistent blocks. With Mark Dees, Timmy McWilliams, and Joe Banasky, we advanced to the playoffs until we again lost to Peary who had handed us a defeat in the regular season.

Mike came of age and the Reed Rebels were formed. In their first season, as we were departing to Sallisaw, the Rebels won the Tulsa City Wide Baseball Championship. Billie and Annice drove Mike back to Tulsa for each game.

Our four years of youth sports in Sallisaw I consider to have been a fine experience for us all. I cannot let it go unnoted.

Keeping in mind no endeavor in life is immune to the critic, there were occasional conflicts. A Sallisaw Public Schools bus driver, Homer Flute, approached me about his son, George, and his nephew, Ricky Joe Fogg, coming from Henderson to play with my team.

Some considered them to be "outsiders," but that was not the view of the substantial majority of their teammates. Parents at times expressed other feelings. Homer had his boys at every game and practice. At times, because of work schedules, the timing was very close. I can still create a mental image of Homer's red pickup truck kicking up a contrail of dust in its wake and kids waving their gloves from the bouncing bed as it raced toward the ball field.

Our committed sponsor, Clayton Farmer, the co-owner of Farmer-O'Neil Ford, after a frank discussion, didn't view the boys' participation as a difficulty despite a complaint or two. Clayton was a calm and inclusive man.

Ultimately, this group would play what I still consider to be the best youth baseball games I have ever seen, and they let me come along for the ride.

We added a fine young pitcher, Ferris Vann, from Bunch just to the north of Henderson. We entered what seemed to be a major tournament in Fort Smith. Physically, Ferris was as frail a boy as I had ever seen. Billie expressed the concern that he might have rickets. His health was excellent and his arm even better, but it was his attitude that was his greatest asset. Although he had been just months too old for our group in Sallisaw, I had worked with him individually as his team practiced. I liked Ferris Vann.

Somewhere in this mix were Freddie Watts, Mike Hight, and Steve Parsons. Steve had a distinctive rally cry, a sound which compelled his teammates to nickname him "Super Chicken." We lost him far too soon.

In the semi-finals, Ferris took the mound against a team from Greenwood, Arkansas. In the third inning, Ferris threw a breaking pitch that didn't break and hit the batter. He was promptly bunted to second. We secured a second out before the next hitter drove a screamer just past Ricky Joe's reach at third to score the runner from second. Greenwood led at the end of three, 1-0.

Ferris went from very good to outstanding. His fast ball and change up hit David's target with great regularity, and the breaking ball was so sharp that David was digging pitches from the dirt that appeared to be approaching at waist height.

We had been putting the ball in play, scratching out a base hit here and there, but Greenwood's fielding was immaculate. Our fielding had matched theirs with Phillip Rhodes, Mike, and Bill Nowlin turning a 6-4-3 double play to end the bottom of the sixth. Finally, in the top of the seventh, Phillip beat out a slow roller. Mike took the first pitch as Phillip stole second then bunted him to third. Then, with a second out recorded, David doubled into left center as Phillip sprinted home with the tying run.

Ferris eased through the bottom of the seventh with the aid of a nice play by Phillip as he ran down a soft fly ball in the hole at short. The game was tied at the end of seven. We headed to extra innings.

Billie and the Boys

The toll of the August heat and the strain of so many meaningful pitches were now rapidly becoming visible. I sat beside Ferris and we talked before I sent him out for the eighth.

He got the first out, then gave up a base hit and threw eight consecutive balls. With the bases loaded and one out, I went to get him. He had nothing left but his desire to win this game. Ferris looked at me with a pleading disappointment. He did not want to give up the ball and in my heart I did not want to take it, but I did. I didn't hug him until we were back in the dugout. I really liked this kid.

David Covington, a tall lanky boy with a rifle arm and shotgun control, came on. With the bases loaded, he threw six pitches. They were bullets that amazed me and him. He secured two strikeouts, getting us out of the inning and on to the ninth. He looked unhittable.

Unfortunately, those six strikes were all that were in his tank that day. To open the bottom of the ninth, he threw twelve straight balls to load the bases.

I stood on the mound, somewhat hoping that George, who was in left field, might look my way, but he didn't. I looked at David. His face was literally flaked with mud from the sweat and the dust of catching the game. He was clearly exhausted. As he took his gear off, I brought the infield in and was adamant in my instructions about a force play at the plate.

I said, "Best you've got left." I handed David the ball and watched him throw a few pitches, then told the umpire, "He's ready."

David found the where-with-all to strike out the first batter. Early in the count, the next boy struck a sharp ground ball to Mike. He came home for one out and the catcher fired the ball to first. Bill stretched mightily for the ball. I thought he held the base, got the runner and got us out of the inning, but the umpire signaled safe.

"Take the easy out." It was what I always said with two outs and runners on.

As well-coached teams do, their runners were on the move at the crack of the bat. A slow roller was hit back to Phillip. He closed quickly and came up cleanly. Judging he couldn't get the runner at home, he looked to first. Then, he just stood helplessly, holding the ball as the winning run scored. A pained look of confusion and frustration covered his face. His teammates engulfed him.

After nine innings played in stifling heat, there was not an error committed by either team in a game that required sound hitting and outstanding defensive plays on crisply struck balls.

It was a truly fine game. I think back on this August day and comprehend it is about the boys and the quality of the endeavor. Their effort on this afternoon will remain one of my measures of excellence.

A youth basketball program did not exist in Sallisaw. Without the assistance of the Sallisaw Superintendent of Schools and an Assistant Football Coach, a team would never have existed.

As good fortune would have it, the Superintendent was my high school football coach, Dick Mosley. During our very early days in Sallisaw, a solid friendship evolved. He made evening gym time available, providing there was a member of the athletic department present. It would have been very easy for him to have said no, but he didn't.

If Dick had not made the executive decision, and had Coach Stanley Collins not generously given of his time, nothing would have happened. Coach Collins, a player's parent and an Assistant Football Coach, went above and beyond in making facilities and equipment available to us. Most importantly, Stanley Collins was a good man.

For two years, I got to be in a gym with our sons and their friends. Burn Collins and Gary Boyd provided talent and a physical play at forward. Bill Nowlin rapidly became a post presence with a willingness to learn that allowed him to become a rebounder to be reckoned with. Phillip Rhodes was as quick and tenacious a shut down defender as I would ever coach. David could manage the floor and shoot the ball. Joe David Davis and Mike Ellis gave us a solid and versatile backup.

We traveled by car with parent drivers, Billie and I in the front seat with a player between us and often four more in the back seat. A high school friend, Jim Parker, had developed a really competitive youth basketball program at Whitefield. The Whitefield experiences were wonderful for my team.

It was a fun time. We won a large number of games and lost a few. It is the practice nights in the gym when everyone could play, improve, listen, and laugh I particularly recall. There was a team trip to Tulsa to watch the University of Tulsa play that was a special outing.

My experiences with these boys remain exceptionally meaningful to me.

CHAPTER THIRTY

Cascia Hall
Fall of 1964

One of the things I really enjoyed about the insurance business was the diverse array of people who would come to comprise a client base. The lessons I learned from my tutors in Hays and Buchanan still served me well. I knew you had to be available. I knew I made no sales in the office nor did I especially like being in confined to my office without the flow of customers coming in and out of the door. So I came to know the coffee break time at a number of larger downtown companies.

Over coffee, I learned of new cars, new houses, and new people being transferred to town. If you take the time to learn what interests a person, you will always have fodder for good conversation. I must say, conversation is considerably more about listening than about talking. I have rarely learned anything when I am doing the talking.

Through contacts provided by a substantial and long-standing Liberty Mutual client base of Amerada Hess employees, I now provided the insurance coverage for several instructors in the Petroleum Engineering Department at the University of Tulsa as clients. I quickly discovered university teachers had a large number of coffee breaks and were on the whole excellent conversation. From this TU tie, I ultimately gained far more than business.

In the fall of 1964, I was offered a nine hour tuition waver. No one took a coffee break before 10, so I enrolled in two early morning classes. One of these was the finest experience I ever had in a history class. It was taught by one of the premiere historians I have ever encountered, Dr. William A. Settle, who taught "The American Frontier."

He was approaching the publication of his seminal work on Jesse James. After class, he enjoyed sharing his knowledge with all who would hang around a bit longer.

I don't remember the second class, but the third turned out not to be the independent study I had thought I had selected but rather an educational observation. I had no interest in professional education or observation. I was disinterested but it was free so I attended the personal conference for the class.

While I can't remember the name of the instructor, he listened to me and, more importantly, he heard me. He asked me what I might contribute to a school. I know I must have told him, "Virtually nothing." I assured him that the two classes would consume all my available time during the school day. He told me to call him back after lunch. I got busy at the office and, being more than a little pessimistic about the possibilities; I did not call back until later in the day.

He asked me if I have ever heard of Cascia Hall. I said, "Kinda." I remember because, saying he was an old high school English teacher, he suggested a grammar correction to me. This was likely the least I deserved for my apathy and tardiness.

He gave me name and telephone of Fr. James J. Sinnott at Cascia Hall, telling me Fr. Sinnott was in need of a volunteer football coach, and if I could work it out, he would be willing to consider that as meeting the requirements of the course.

A few springs prior, Coach Spilsbury had reignited my interest in football, so I thought, "What the hell. I'll stop by on the way home and meet the man." I wondered if Catholic Priests needed automobile insurance.

At first, Cascia Hall seemed little more than an intriguing architectural anomaly. Constructed of irregular bricks and a tower entrance with an immense double door, this place gave me a sense of medieval foreboding. The heavy doors required some effort to open them. I'm certain I expected the door to make some eerie creaking sound as I pulled it open.

The spiraling marble staircase with its forged iron rail seemed out of place and time. Its location was physically close to a downtown Tulsa, a downtown that was filling in its spaces between its beautiful art deco buildings from earlier periods of prosperity with shiny new glass walled structures. Cascia Hall seemed set apart even in that eclectic cityscape.

Upon entry into the silent hallway, a glance to the right revealed the Office of the Headmaster. Now, I wasn't certain what a Headmaster was. Feeling awkwardly out of place, I was giving strong consideration to simply calling it a day and going home for a little pre-dinner backyard baseball with the boys.

I might have left had a very affable Jane Stafford not appeared in the doorway and said, "Mr. McBride?" I nodded or something. She finished, "Father is expecting you."

His thinning hair and his brushy eyebrows both appeared darker than nature alone might have provided, but as the popular saying of the time went, "he could sell you swamp land in Florida." The Very Reverend James J. Sinnott was most warm and welcoming. Our conversation was pleasant and informative, and the gentleman from TU had already whispered the magic words into Father's ear: "He'd be free."

After something of an interview, Father Sinnott said I was quite acceptable to him, but he wanted me to visit with the football coach, Bill Hamill, before a final commitment. Father walked to the door with me and directed me down the covered walkway toward Chestnut Gym.

The coaches' dressing room was down a few steps and in the basement of the gym. With its wooden lockers and large nail hangers, it felt and smelled a great deal like the semi-basement dressing room in the WPA gym in Stigler. It smelled like high school athletics. Given the proper pleasant association, an odor becomes a fragrance.

Coach Hamill and Frank Hagedorn, a student at the University Of Tulsa School Of Law and the assistant football coach, were just finishing changing after coming in from the practice field.

We talked, and Coach Hamill found me acceptable and somewhere along the way, a lifelong friendship took root.

The football experience was everything Coach Spilsbury had promised me it would be. Some years later, in my office at Cascia Hall, I would caution a young man whose parents were quite apprehensive about his expressions of interest in becoming a

Billie and the Boys

football coach. I discussed competitive euphoria and the addictive properties of coaching football with him. Joey Medina followed his path to football and it led him back to Cascia Hall.

Yes, in the final game of the 1964 season, Cascia Hall did score twice in the final 27 seconds to defeat Bishop Kelley. To me, the most memorable element of that final play was Charlie McNamara getting up after his initial block and peeling a pursuing defender from Steve Cullinan's back to allow him to find Terry Malloy alone in the end zone while three Kelley defenders draped themselves around Dickie Allred.

Bill Hamill moved to Houston for a job with NASA. I moved on with my career in the insurance business.

A couple of years later, we got a telephone call from Bill telling us of his decision to enter the Priesthood. This prompted Billie to declare, "My God, next you'll tell me there's no Santa Claus!"

In the summer of 1970, Angelo Prassa and Fr. Bernie Flynn convinced me that coming to Cascia Hall to coach and teach while attending graduate school at The University of Tulsa was the most viable path to walk. Prior to their offer, it had been my intent to remain in Sallisaw and commute to graduate school in Fayetteville. Billie and I discussed the option of remaining in Sallisaw. The decision was not simple.

We sat on the steps of the house we had rented at the corner of 20th and Xanthus, awaiting the arrival of the truck from Sallisaw. We verbally wondered if there was any way we could just contact the moving van somewhere on the Muskogee Turnpike and turn it around. Had it been this age of cell phones when fleeting impulses can be acted upon, I wonder if we would have actually made such a telephone call and missed this life we love so much.

It is what it is.

Deoch an doruis

www.ingramcontent.com/pod-product-compliance
Lightning Source LLC
Chambersburg PA
CBHW031642040426
42453CB00006B/189